The Normandy Diary
of
Marie-Louise Osmont:
1940–1944

THE NORMANDY DIARY

of

MARIE-LOUISE OSMONT: 1940–1944

Marie-Louise Osmont

INTRODUCTION BY
John Keegan

TRANSLATED BY
George L. Newman

RANDOM HOUSE / THE DISCOVERY CHANNEL PRESS

ACKNOWLEDGEMENTS

The diary of Marie-Louise Osmont was discovered and preserved by
the city of Caen and the Memorial Caen Normandie.

Illustrations and maps by Gerald Quinn.

Special thanks to Kim Chaix and Chris Koch.

Foreword by Rebecca Farwell.

Library of Congress Cataloging in Publication
data is available.

ISBN 0-679-43438-0

Book design by Charles Ziga, Ziga Design

Manufactured in the United States of America

2 4 6 8 9 5 3

First Edition

I f you travel north toward the sea on a small, winding road from Caen, you'll come to the village of Périers, folded into rolling farmland. At the heart of this village is Château Périers, and in this house lived Marie-Louise Osmont.

She was born Marie-Louise Mignard in Paris in May 1890. Her parents moved to Pau, a town in southwestern France, where Marie-Louise eventually attended nursing school. After graduating in 1912, she signed up with the Red Cross, and when war broke out, she volunteered for an army medical unit on the front.

Three years later, she received a letter ordering her to come to Paris with her nursing papers and "one trunk not exceeding 30 kilograms." She was assigned to the Central Hospital in Bar-le-Duc, where the worst of the war wounded were brought. She drove an ambulance back and forth from the front and assisted the chief surgeons, who wrote in the margins of her service record that she was "a perfect nurse in every respect" and exhibited "dedication beyond praise." A final entry notes that she "rendered the highest service"; it is signed by a consulting surgeon named Osmont.

After the war, Dr. Osmont took his new wife home to his Normandy village of Périers. He was fifty-seven; she was twenty-eight. Marie-Louise found herself in the middle of a well-established community. Dr. Osmont employed a maid, a gardener, a cook (the gardener's wife), and tenant farmers, a family of six who had worked there for years, taking out nine-year leases at a time. Some of them were suspicious of this self-confident newcomer, but the demands of the seasons, around which the château revolved, soon drew Marie-Louise into the center of château life.

Château Périers, in turn, was the center of village life. It was surrounded by vegetable gardens, flower gardens, and carefully groomed beds of cyclamens, roses, irises, and lilies. The lawns were shaded by hemlock and birch trees, a prized American walnut, and an ancient platan that sloughed great heaps of bark every year. The tenant farmer and his son raised dairy cows, sheep, horses, chickens, and goats, and tilled vast fields of crops. There was a house for making cheese, a stone room for curing meat, a blacksmith shop, and a greenhouse — warmed in the winter by hot-water pipes — in which Marie-Louise cultivated grapes for raisins.

Dr. Osmont introduced his bride to old friends of the family in nearby Mathieu. Marie-Louise became quite close to them. The Osmonts developed a warm circle of friends in Caen as well, and spent many evenings there dining and going to the theater. They also entertained at home. The house itself was a tall, sturdy rectangle, substantial without being grand. White shutters and pale stucco gave the façade an open, friendly mien. Inside, the floors and the large central stairway were laid with soft, smooth stone quarried in Caen. The heavy slate roof was insulated with dirt from the gardens, and a fireplace stretched the width of the kitchen, with a brick oven built in for baking bread.

As she settled in, Madame Osmont hung tapestries and filled armoires, collecting things that turned each room into a reflection of herself. From anywhere in the house, she could look upon her gardens and trees and the wall that encircled the house, built of stones turned up in the fields. In this home, constructed of the land itself, she put down her roots. She and Dr. Osmont lived together here for nearly twenty years until his death in 1937. She buried him in the churchyard a short walk away.

From Périers, Marie-Louise would ride her bicycle along the country lanes to the shore, to Mathieu, and beyond, or race around the countryside in her treasured car, a Rosengart, propelled by enthusiasm and a heavy foot—the unbreakable habit, perhaps, of a former ambulance driver. She kept constantly busy and refused to hide her contempt for those she found less industrious—endearing herself to some and estranging herself from others. She intimidated many adults and children, though she was tenderly devoted to the daughter of a friend, a young nurse who worked at a Catholic hospital in Caen. Madame Osmont doted on her dogs and spent hours outdoors with them. Friends—"the old gang," as she called them—came and went through her open doorway.

In 1940, the year Hitler invaded France, Madame Osmont was a widow, overseeing the château herself, working in the library in Caen, and volunteering for the Red Cross, a devotion born of vocation and of war. One August day, strangers appeared at her door: six German aviators with a requisition slip to occupy the château. They would stay, but so would she.

Despite the presence of German and then British soldiers, despite the trucks in her garden and the bombs in her fields, Marie-Louise endeavored to "create in this topsy-turvy universe a spot, however small, of peace, harmony, and beauty." To her, the château was more than a shelter: "This house…has been in turn my despair, my worry, my refuge," she would write. "From it I get something like a magic spell: I feel myself in intimate communion with it. What powers could these old stones have, what secret energy could have been left by the departed who once lived here?" Through occupation and bombardment, invasion and liberation, Marie-Louise Osmont would defend her home, one tiny part of France.

This is her diary of those years.

TRANSLATOR'S NOTE

I wish that the reader could have peered over my shoulder while I translated *The Normandy Diary of Marie-Louise Osmont*. Looking at the handwritten original, you would have seen how certain entries were made just after the events they describe, while other passages were added later—in the margins or on the backs of pages— during periods of relative calm, when Madame Osmont was able to think about and flesh out her story. For the purpose of readability, these margin notes have been incorporated into each entry here; still, both Marie-Louise Osmont's terror and her reflective nature are recognizable.

Four short passages were blacked out in the original diary, whether by the author or by someone else, and for what reason we will never know. These have been deleted from the text. The names of all French citizens—except for Madame Osmont, her husband, and public figures—have been changed, in accordance with French law.

Tucked between the pages of the diary was Madame Osmont's glossary of the Franco-German "language," which gives her humorous view of the German soldiers' slang—a mixture of German, French, and even English. (See page 114.) Her frequent use of German and English words provided some interesting puzzles; although her French grammar and spelling are impeccable, the same cannot be said of her attempts to transcribe foreign words phonetically (her use of German and English words are preserved here in italics). Her inconsistent spelling of words such as *Spiess* have been corrected, but some transcription errors, such as the British battleship *Ramillies*, which Osmont spelled *Ramili*, have been preserved. I am grateful to members of CompuServe's Military and Foreign Language forums for help in solving these and other mysteries of Madame Osmont's diary, which enabled me to provide the translation notes at the back of the book.

Madame Osmont's description of the sound made by passing or incoming artillery shells presented a different sort of mystery. The word that she uses—*siffler*—can mean "hiss" or "whistle," or something in between; how to translate it? I am indebted to World War II veterans Charles Dean and John Parry, who did their best to describe it to me.

Finally, I want to express my deepest appreciation to Marie-Laurence Wax, whose help in deciphering the diarist's handwriting averted untold misreadings on my part, and whose suggestions added immeasurably to the translation.

— George L. Newman

INTRODUCTION

How fascinating that this diary of D-Day and the Battle of Normandy has come to light and been published in English in time for the fiftieth anniversary of the campaign for Europe's liberation. It is a unique document. Marie-Louise Osmont witnessed the landing of the Allied troops from her family home, which stands only three miles inland from Sword Beach, at the center of the invasion front. In the weeks before D-Day she was forced to accept a large party of the German defenders of the Atlantic Wall as billeted lodgers. A few days after June 6 her house and outbuildings were full of British liberators, whose arrival had brought heavy damage to the château's cherished structure and killed or wounded many of her friends and neighbors. She herself was wounded in the exchanges of fire that opened the fight for the foothold.

We can identify precisely both the units, German and British, that intruded into Marie-Louise Osmont's peaceful, everyday life and many of the incidents of fighting that engulfed her house. Château Périers stands in the village Périers-sur-le-Dan on a by-road that runs from Caen, the departmental capital of Calvados, to Luc-sur-Mer, an initial objective of the British 3rd Infantry Division. The sector was defended by the German 716th Infantry Division, a "static" (*bodenstandige*) formation, whose role was to hold the blockhouses and trenches of the coastline "to the last man and the last round." Its soldiers were either elderly or juvenile, and included numbers of non-Germans, swept up into the Wehrmacht because of the manpower crisis brought on by the grievous losses suffered on the Eastern Front. Badly equipped and without transport, it had no capacity for maneuver or counterattack. Its soldiers knew that their task was to stand fast on the Atlantic Wall or die in the attempt.

The British troops Madame Osmont came to know after her unhappy German visitors had been killed or captured in defense of Périers were Royal Marine Commandos of 42nd, 43rd, and 47th Commando, which formed the 4th Special Service Brigade and landed on Sword Beach in the first wave. They were an elite, young, fit, highly trained, and superbly equipped for the assault role. Quite unlike their German opponents, they brimmed with self-confidence and were buoyed with the sense of fighting for a just cause on the winning side.

Our awareness of this contrast makes Madame Osmont's observations of the differences between her German and British visitors all the more intriguing. She did not dislike all the Germans she met and she did dislike a few of the British. The ordinary German soldiers often aroused her pity. They were fearful and unenthusiastic warriors, who reduced themselves to tears when they showed her photographs of their wives and children; the imminence of death was heavy upon them. She was also touched by their singing, which was "melancholy but so musical." Her British marines bawled out untunefully any old song that suited their mood. Nevertheless, with them she felt in the presence of people of free spirit. They conveyed "a gaiety expressed in constant songs—not harmonious perhaps, but suggesting youth or freedom from care; whistles, calls, and certainly jokes that I don't understand. Free men who seem to be enjoying themselves. I think of the grave young Germans, sad and mechanical, of their rare songs...So many differences between these two peoples. We seem to be closer to the English."

She was a keen observer of national differences, and quickly spotted the "milord" manners that characterized the British even at the height of the desperate Normandy battle. Her château became an officers' mess for a headquarters. "At two o'clock, arrival of my new guests: loaded trucks, unpacking of an enormous amount of equipment, setting up the kitchen, the dining room for *messieurs* the officers, and their lounge in the parlor. Deafening noise, commotion, singing, laughing, shouting, various jokes, almost like southerners. I am dumbfounded. I didn't think the English were so demonstrative. But what an army! A gong is sounded for tea and for lunch, and at five o'clock, with all work over for practical purposes, the officers are settled into easy chairs, reading. I have the feeling that I'm housing a large restaurant for 'gentlemen'…barely a month ago I still had the others…and what a difference in their conceptions of war."

Since the German army took war seriously and the British, who thought war was an extension of sport, did not, it was ironic that the Germans were losing the battle of Normandy. Madame Osmont, though she was unaware of it, witnessed one of the most crucial episodes of the whole Normandy battle, the counterattack of 21st Panzer Division on the evening of D-Day. The panzers had been ordered to drive to the beaches and their corps commander, General Bronikowski, warned, "If you do not succeed in pushing the British back into the sea, I'm afraid we have lost the war." At eight o'clock on the evening of D-Day the tanks of 21st Panzer Division reached the 716th Division's positions just beyond Périers. But, lacking support, they did not press home their attack and eventually withdrew. That may, indeed, have been the moment at which D-Day succeeded.

In the aftermath of the failed German counterattack, Madame Osmont meets two soldiers of the 716th Division she knew from the pre-invasion period. "You feel that these two men are lost, disoriented, sad. Later, almost night, I see them again, their faces deliberately blackened with charcoal, crossing the park. What will be their fate? How many of them are still in the area, hiding and watching?" Later she meets others who have been taken prisoner, and are exhausted and terrified by the ordeal of battle. She — and some British soldiers — give them tea and crackers and jam, on which they fall famished. The reversal of roles is absolute. The occupied and liberators feel pity for the German enemy, who are almost euphoric with happiness at their release from the threat of extinction.

This wonderful diary abounds with vignettes. Deeply religious, Madame Osmont records every mass she attends, is impressed by the piety of the British soldiers who take part, then notes that an officer who takes communion also carefully loots something he needs from her home. The Germans, though extortionate, had given receipts for everything they took. The British regard her château as open house, shooting locks off doors to rob her of her possessions, some of which she later retrieves from ditches where they have been discarded. She records a little scene where General Montgomery distributes medals to his soldiers. He is "plain, [his] face thin and delicate, body rather skinny, black beret, few gestures, no stiff attitude, no apparent arrogance, probably nice." She mourns for neighbors killed in the fighting, helpless victims of bombardment of their homes or farms, some killed in the field as they try to get in the harvest. She records the death of cattle killed in their stalls. She gives a home to a stray dog, which becomes a cherished friend.

At the end, as the battle ebbs away toward the Seine, and Paris is about to be liberated, she walks the fields of conflict. She visits the château of a neighbor, gutted by fire, and finds "at the end of the garden two cemeteries, one English, one German: names and dates, helmets and crosses. On one German cross the dates of birth and death indicate a child of nineteen years." Madame Osmont is gifted with great powers of observation and description and imbued with profound qualities of pity and compassion. Her diary leaves us with a record for which there is no equivalent for the battle of Normandy, and very few from the whole history of warfare. What would we give for a similar diary by a countrywoman whose house had stood on the front line between Union and Confederacy outside Richmond in 1864, a German diary of the battle of Berlin, a Russian diary from

Stalingrad, a British diary from the Indian mutiny? Marie-Louise Osmont bears comparison with "Missie" Vassilchikov or Christabel Bielenberg, and her journal is destined to become part of the universal literature of conflict.

—JOHN KEEGAN

THE NORMANDY DIARY
of
MARIE-LOUISE OSMONT:
1940–1944

August 6, 1940

First occupation of the Château de Périers by the Germans; altogether, two non-commissioned officers and four enlisted men.

It seems terrible—for me they represent Invasion, Defeat. Seeing these six booted aviators move into three rooms (gray bedroom and small library room, left side as you go upstairs, and large room with two beds on the right side), I am heartbroken. The house (although by now I no longer have a maid) is spotlessly clean, polished up, each rare curio in its place, flowers in the vases. The garden is still pretty to look at, in spite of the fact that Antoine the gardener has left, a prisoner; there are flowers, vegetables, and fruit.

I find these six men extremely irritating, except for a certain Franz (from near the Dutch border), really very young and charming. As a matter of fact, they are all six well bred, discreet, and clean. They spend the whole day in their underwear, which is unaesthetic but not really malicious; they make noise, which is natural; they don't have much to eat, and Bernice makes them omelettes and fried potatoes with their purchases. They have almost no work to do, play cards. Young Franz follows me around like a puppy while I do the housework and jabbers bad French incessantly. He wants to teach me German and thinks that he knows French.

All six seem almost like waifs.

One day they asked me to let them come to the parlor at eight o'clock in the evening, to listen to a special radio broadcast for the German soldiers—I almost said no, that was my first impulse. Nevertheless I agreed. Each day they knock on the door at the precise time and settle in near the radio while I pretend to be intent on my knitting. One of them offers me an "English cigarette" (they deliberately emphasize). After listening, they leave again with profuse thanks. Well bred, discreet...and their presence is unbearable to me! (I have often thought of them since probably all killed—in the midst of the confusion, the filth, and the screams.)

August 15, 1940

An infantry officer, haughty, came to visit, relegated the six (annoyed) aviators to two rooms, and ordered me to empty the place of nearly everything except the immovable furniture: dining room, parlor, study, and part of the third floor; I still have my bedroom, along with the dressing room and the little boudoir.

I cried. Frantic and desperate, I moved all the pretty little fragile furniture to the third floor, into two bedrooms, hid the small treasures, the brasses, everything that seemed precious to me. I spent the afternoon and night at it.

The next morning, a company marching as if on parade made a circuit of the lawn and, on command, stacked their weapons in front of the house. I was overcome with emotion; so many things went through my mind! Fifty-two men in the house, Bavarians and Prussians. Indeed I quarreled with them all; I complained more than once. I was restless and light-headed with the spirit of battle, wanting to defend this house at any price. I was, above all else, desperate.

August 17, 1940

The big oak table from the dining room was carried into the garden. The clerk settled in, making check marks in his record books, then medics armed with pads and iodine, and finally the medical officer. A procession of more than one hundred bare-chested men, coming to be vaccinated against typhoid.

August 18, 1940

Small bombardment, not very far away, by airplane. Excitement among the men; the officer, still aloof, has trenches dug in the enclosed garden and the chicken coop (after long study to find the best place).

Departure of the six aviators.

Night alert drill and practicing rapid departure by truck. The truck bumps the right gatepost and knocks it to the ground (gate sprung and can no longer be closed). Repeated protests and complaints on my part. The Germans, after long examinations by the brass, put the post back up themselves (crooked).

I complain about the soldiers who are ransacking the vegetable garden. They are made to line up in two ranks in front of the stoop, and I go among them to identify and point them out. I'm rather nervous. One of them shows me a photo of a bombed-out house, telling me that "soon the château will look like this." I answer, "With you in it, so much the better." He answers I don't know what, looking nasty, while talking about "grapes." I was to understand later that he had stolen the grapes from the greenhouse. It's been like this for a month—an uneasy life, nights without sleep because of the noise, the repulsive filth of the garden and the house, the wretched staircase ravaged by hobnails, furniture full of jam and soup, men eating just about everywhere and throwing what they don't like on the floor. In the park one steps in...despite a special ditch dug under the trees.

The village has some of them in nearly every house.

September 15, 1940

Finally, they leave one night, taking their equipment (mattresses, blankets) with them. The greenhouse is ransacked, the panes broken, probably by the soldier with the photo.

October 12, 1940

German airplane shot down and catches fire on the ground at the Montblanc farm.

March 19, 1942

Four Germans to house for four days; officer almost invisible, men well behaved; a huge Bavarian, rather funny. No trouble.

Crashed at Périers: an English airplane in Lignoir's garden, still another in Montblanc's pasture.

_____ **1942**

Is it quieter? Or am I going to get used to this state of affairs? It's gotten so that I meet the men, around the former lawn, almost without seeing them. They themselves seem almost happy, probably relieved when they compare themselves to those who are fighting. Sometimes they show me photos of comrades who have been killed. I've learned to shrug my shoulders and say, *"C'est la guerre"* [that's war], as they themselves do, even though it's horrible!

_____ **1943**

House occupied by units whose sole occupation is to scribble ceaselessly on tons of paper and type. They are perhaps alarming, but quiet. Nothing picturesque. It's like living in a ministry (or an embassy). (Not much to eat; I'm hungry.)

_____ **1943**

Met a man in the park, who had already spoken to me in almost-correct French. I ask him the name of the unit that's staying at my house and blackening so much paper. He puts a finger to his lips as a signal for silence, then with great mystery he says, "Police." —?? That doesn't tell me anything new — what's odd is that they know my maiden name! What good does that do them??

Bernice contrives to cook nettles in the style of chopped spinach; it isn't bad, but without any fat, it's certainly not very nourishing! I drink a lot of water several times a day; it quiets the rumbling of my stomach...I'm hungry...

February 9, 1944, Wednesday evening
I was staying at Caen. After dinner I went to the Rue de Geöle, to the Montards' house. They were shattered. The order had arrived to evacuate "immediately and without delay" the entire Château de Mathieu, including the outbuildings, and to turn over the vegetable garden. Huge house, occupied by the family ever since the Beauchamps grandparents, where over the years they have amassed antique furniture, small collectors' items, the thousand objects needed by a large family, to say nothing of the enormous collection of archives, books, and scientific documents accumulated by Mr. Lignoir. House full of memories, full of the past.

I'm devastated. I understand and share their distress. For twenty years my life has run close to theirs, at times mixing with it. I respect them, I love them; they are like family. They decide to get everything out, to gather everything together in Caen, to do anything in order to keep the vegetable garden, which helps them live. Sleepless night. I think of them, and I fear for myself; I ask myself whether, if I faced the same fate, I would have the same quiet courage.

February 11, 1944, Friday
Two mornings later, I go to Mathieu to try—along with so many others—to help them if possible. It's heartbreaking to see this house being emptied. Around eleven o'clock in the morning, in the middle of everybody's hurried coming and going, I hear the telephone ring in the hall. I'm nearby. I grab it. I hear Bernice's panic-stricken voice calling, "Madame," because ten of these gentlemen are inspecting Périers in order to occupy it. I answer, "I'm on my way." I jump on my bicycle, and in spite of a terrible, icy wind, I rush down the road. Car parked in front of the gate, group of officers and junior officers stopped in the little path, conferring with Bernice and the mayor. I come up to them, I greet the officer with a "Good day, sir,"

which I intend to be correct and which is probably icy. They tell me that they are going to billet men in the house. I ask whether I can keep my bedroom. They answer, "Of course," almost good-naturedly, as if it's the most natural thing in the world. My heart beats a little slower. They reinspect the different rooms, which they have done already in my absence. I go past my side, which is still locked, saying, "That is my room, sir." They don't ask to see it! By evening, everything has to be clear—that is to say the ground floor (except for the study, where I will pile the furniture), the second floor except for my side, the third floor except for the end bedroom and the big attic. They parley in front of the outbuildings, ask me to remove the car, to which I reply that it's impossible. They leave.

Working until the middle of the night (with the help of Bernice and Pierre), I emptied all the rooms of their contents, except for the bulky, immovable armoires.

I packed away as many things as possible, something I had never done before. The experience proved to me that I had not yet emptied out enough. I was supposed to give them absolutely bare rooms.

Around ten o'clock in the evening, a cariloe[1] arrives. Two soldiers unload vegetables, bread, a Frigidaire, and begin to set themselves up in the dining room.

A non-commissioned officer of the *Kommandantur* [headquarters] arrives, sets up some crates in the parlor, carefully and mysteriously locks up, and asks me for a room.

February 12, 1944, in the morning

Six-ton trucks and yet more six-ton trucks, continually unloading in front of the house, on the grass, in the park, an unexpected and disturbing array of equipment. Where can they put all that? I try to talk to them, but I get nothing definite. I understand only (and very clearly) that they have decided to squeeze everything in, and my heart stops, since I am terribly afraid that they might tell me to empty the premises.

February 13, 1944

More trucks, now with the addition of carts, livestock carts, wagons. All of them full to overflowing: mattresses, beds, armoires, Louis XII armchairs, leather armchairs, mirrors, washbasins, bathtubs (stolen from just about everywhere), corrugated metal, timber, coal, potatoes, cases of ammunition, etc., etc.

I go through a succession of unpleasant emotions: panic, anger, dumb resignation, discouragement, with a kind of physical fatigue: rubbery legs, nausea, intense cold. It's hard having to fight alone, and yet it's so much better this way!

I realize, nevertheless, that I have become inured to it and that if, at the beginning of 1940, I had seen the invasion of the house taking this form, I would have suffered far more! One really does get used to many things. I also think that all this is beyond me, that I only have the will to fight for the little things, and especially to look like the proprietor, the landlady who wants to show that she is there...but that's all. The fate of this property is no longer in my hands; we are in the midst of chaos—heading toward a near and terrible unknown, and the preservation of rare furniture, antique tapestries, fragile curios, all that seems ridiculous. I will fight for the memory of the dead. I will fight largely out of sentimentality, a little bit out of habit, but without conviction, and that is perhaps what makes me the saddest. Neither enthusiasm nor faith in the future...where are we headed? "It is not at all necessary to hope in order to undertake, nor to succeed in order to persevere."

February 14, 1944

Same invading tide. I must turn over to them the outbuildings, the old damp cellars, full of the unspeakable rubbish that one keeps, not knowing why. Also the two rooms called the coachman's rooms, and that's not all: The attics are next! At the idea of having to empty this jumble of boxes, boards, broken furniture, tools of every sort, Bernice loses control and I am very near to doing the same. I wonder whether we aren't going to go crazy, and this morning will remain in my memory as a horrible time.

The second lieutenant had told me that he was going to give me two men to help me. Two civilians arrived, two Russians, one of whom spoke French marvelously and was profuse in his declarations of devotion, his manners as courtly as those of a great lord. He presented himself as a prince or a count! (I don't know which)! Originally from the Ukraine, former owner of a large estate, former court chauffeur, his mother a former lady-in-waiting to the empress (!?). According to him, he was tortured by the Bolsheviks, his family shot, he himself imprisoned, tied up with ropes, etc., etc. His companion, an ex-colonel of lancers (!?). Both of them in rags, dirty but, it must be admitted, with a polish and manners that suggested an origin well above the ordinary. That can't be improvised.

The self-styled prince helped give me a foretaste of madness. He advised me to leave, to flee, promised me the worst misfortunes, gave me atrocious details of today's Russia, predicted a deplorable future for the country. All that in a low voice, mysteriously, a finger to his lips. I came back to my room worn out and terrified. During the day, I got his civilian comrades to talk about him and learned that he had been interned for three years in an insane asylum. That explains quite a few things. Now I listen to him calmly; he amuses me, but from another point of view I don't trust him.

The ex-colonel of lancers has also been mad, it seems (what a pair);

he is short, slight, and wears a little jacket of the Eton type, tight and too short, in which he is bound to shiver.

For this new invasion includes more than just German troops. We are in the very Tower of Babel: Parisian drivers (former taxi or delivery truck drivers) —pure Parisian accent, indescribable slang, a bit rough, but nice. Russians (most of them White Russians): sophisticated, polite, and disturbing; one of them, named Nicholas, has loafed around Paris almost all his life (thirty-two years), making cocktails at the Casanova, also as a taxi driver; indiscreet, impudent as the devil, very funny, but to be put in his place when necessary. Italians: prisoners of war; carried out the occupation of Monte Carlo and Nice, taken prisoner at the time of the armistice and the Italian betrayal (the second one); they're emaciated, sad, sluggish, and shivering; they're half starved. I have discovered an Armenian who comes from Constantinople, stranded here by I don't know what odd circumstance!

It's quite strange, all this mixture of races. It's interesting to observe, worrisome, because all of them steal to improve an abnormal and deplorable existence, and when you consider the return in terms of work, it's absolutely nil. One wonders why the Germans encumber themselves this way, with men who, consistently, do not want to do anything.

—French paid 130 francs a day: they joke, laugh, don't respect the N.C.O.;[2] finagling, making the best of it.

—Russians very ably *pretend* to work.

—Italians: nothing; roll a wheelbarrow when they have no choice or wash a vehicle from time to time.

Another side of the matter: French women (and what women!!) come from seven o'clock in the morning to three o'clock in the afternoon to peel vegetables. Shouts, laughter, blatant behavior! One is ashamed, but that's how it is! Peeling potatoes is certainly not their principal occupation!

Unsuccessful attempt to move the Ciney stove from the parlor; it spends the night outside. In the morning it has disappeared. With the help of an Austrian who speaks French well, I complain. It's the Italians who have taken it. In the afternoon I see it come back on a wagon.

February 15, 1944

One of the women knocks at my door to ask me for sheets of paper for "the gentlemen." Moreover, she has an escort, and I hear muffled laughter behind the door. She introduces herself: "I am one of the kitchen ladies." If anyone had told me before that I would see that in the stairwell (I'm talking about the girl)…

There was also "that thing": a framed picture on the second floor— a life-size Hitler!!! Horrors! It stayed in the stairwell for twenty-four hours, in the place of honor on the chest of drawers. Disappeared. Fortunately, Hitler lasted only a short time at my house. I met an enlisted man, a peasant type, who is leaving the *Kommandantur*. He looked at me with a grand gesture toward the photo, puffed out his lips, and let out a "pffft" of disgust…there were at least two of us with the same opinion!

The second evening of the move, quarter to midnight, I wasn't asleep. Laughter and singing from two men arriving late, probably drunk. Two calls, one right after the other, and a rifle shot. Silence on the road and hubbub in the house. It was the guard posted at the gate who fired. Very distressing feeling, to think that perhaps a man is lying dead. The next morning I learn that it involved two Parisian drivers coming back to sleep at the farm. The bullet barely missed one of them. The guard was apparently trembling with fear!

There is also, all night long, a patrol that changes every three hours. A German escorted by a Frenchman, on whom they put a green overcoat, go around through the park, the garden, around the trucks and the house. For the moment, nothing to fear from the "terrorists."

Seven Matford four-seater cars are parked behind the house in good order. But that's not enough: In the grass sloping down from the vegetable garden, they are going to dig large, deep recesses to shelter them (from what?). As to the six-ton trucks, they showed up first at the park, hiding under the trees, driving over the cyclamens (how sad!). One of them was even hidden under the roses, along the wall; it drove over the stalks of irises and lilies! Two became very nicely stuck in the spongy grass under the American walnut. An entire morning to get them out, with the help of metal gratings, and wasting quite a bit of gasoline.

February 16, 1944, morning

Mornings being always propitious for brilliant inspirations and vast plans, they decide first to put the trucks in the woods, then, a few hours later (orders and counterorders, the military life), in the drive. Great idea! "If you please, madame"; someone leads me politely in front of the gate. Explanations: They're going to remove the markers, they'll knock down the embankment, they'll make a ramp by piling up gravel on each side, under the trees. They'll dig (well, sure!), they'll repile gravel (why not?) and they'll put the trucks in place. In 1940, '41, '42, if anyone had told me that, I would have been shattered; it was what I dreaded the most. Today I listen with perhaps a vague, tight-lipped smile.

February 17, 1944

Execution of this martial project.

Since it rained torrents the whole night, the path that circles what used to be the lawn has become, thanks to the many convoys, a mudhole as deep as a stream; water, liquid mud, a vile sludge. Some Russians are given the job of breaking up the stones of a small wall bordering the old pond, which was knocked down several months ago (I expected to have it put back up one day). These stones are carried in wheelbarrows, some into the deep rut, some onto the former lawn (on which the vehicles have in any case been driving for several days).

I ask the sergeant not to take down walls on the property to find the necessary materials.

Very nicely, he promises me they won't and explains to me that he will "find some in Périers."

In fact it is Mrs. Deforge's wall that is called to the sacrifice (it wasn't used for anything anyway, and was nothing but a ruin). Men take it down, and requisitioned carts carry it here, to make an entry into the drive and a solid path to the site laid out for the trucks.

February 18, 1944

Continued: They work without enthusiasm and without energy.

The second floors of the outbuildings are lit by electricity (they must be pretty astonished). An aluminum wire, badly insulated, brings the current directly from the road (no question of a meter).

It burst into flames today, in one of the coachman's rooms. Someone made a fire in the fireplace, embers fell onto the very old floor. A hole of two square meters is left; the cellar underneath, full of straw, narrowly escaped. The soldiers, rather annoyed, repair it, and I make a few comments.

It will all burst into flames one day; that will settle the question undecided for years: whether or not to destroy these decrepit, unhealthy, and inconvenient outbuildings…

February 19, 1944, Saturday

They continue to work in moderation; they aren't straining themselves. It will stop at noon, in any case, with rest in the afternoon. Sunday, too; I can therefore leave unconcerned for Caen, to come back Sunday evening. It has snowed; icy wind.

I'm dumbfounded to learn that the cook is a "shopkeeper." A Russian explains to me that he sells meat, butter, cognac, etc., to soldiers who want to send packages to their families or take some when they go on leave. He intends to buy some meat from him this very evening, to cook in his room. Will there come a day of great scarcity and very great hunger, suppressing any other feelings, when I will go, with my shopping basket, to buy meat at the door of "my" kitchen?? The irony of fate!! What will we see yet?

February 20, 1944

Saturday evening in Caen. Theater, to change my outlook. Le Regain plays Cinna; unusual sets and costumes, good interpretation. We shivered. Sunday, restaurant lunch with the old gang. Terrifically depressing! I leave at five o'clock in the afternoon; I arrive at Périers pierced through by this Siberian wind. I notice that the big gravel freshly placed around the lawn is thoroughly flattened. No more trucks around the house! Bernice appears and tells me about this bewildering departure: Announced late Saturday evening, the departure took place in good order at ten o'clock in the morning. Destination: Isigny or Carentan (?). Purpose unknown, of course. No more six-ton trucks, no more Matfords, no more Parisian drivers with their Montmartre gab, no more strange-looking Russian civilians. All that's left is the *Kommandantur* and its associated services: tack room in the outbuildings, cobbler on the third floor tapping constantly; tailor, barracks of soldiers in the parlor, and the kitchen—quiet, actually; the field kitchen has left as well.

After the insane hubbub of the past week, the house seems empty. Silence, no coming and going, a rest home for pensioners...Bernice, who had of course already established lots of relationships among the French and Russian drivers, is almost sad!! Incredible! And her husband is a prisoner...

The whole area around the house is clean and freshly picked up. They have taken away a lot of equipment; bathtubs and washbasins have disappeared (where to?), the gasoline depot is gone, the timber taken up.

They have also taken the rubber watering hose that the sergeant had asked me for and which, although in bad condition, belonged to me just the same. It's a small point.

We still have remaining, neatly stacked, the corrugated metal and, thank God, the enormous depot of cases of ammunition; we can defend ourselves or blow up, take your pick.

A peaceful evening by the fireside. At nine-thirty the electricity goes out, the fuses must have blown. Someone knocks at my door, twice, tries to open the door. I hesitate — uncertain, I don't move. They'll have to learn to get through the night without me. Ten minutes later, the lights come back on; they've found the meter.

February 21, 1944, Monday

Gray, cold day; nothing special.

Big decrease in the comings and goings in the second-floor stairwell. Someone comes to see the officer in a pretty four-wheeled phaetontype carriage, two bay horses, nice harness. Style.

I go to ask the mayor to see that I am provided with a requisition slip.[3] He would prefer, naturally, that I request it myself. I tell him that since he has directed the requisitioning in this area, it is up to him to do it and not me, a poor requisitionee. Then, too, he is the mayor; it's his "job." But he is a timid man, even a coward.

February 22, 1944

Apart from a violent and icy wind, dead quiet in the house. If this continues I may think I'm in a convent.

Quiet — minimum of noise — peaceful nights. I sleep like lead — except for the nightmares.

February 25, 1944

Don't trust the kitchen women.

The officer goes away on leave. A young N.C.O. (?) comes to inspect, he's twenty years old. Everybody's heels clicking.

February 26, 1944

Visit to second floor of the outbuildings, transformed into repair shop and equipment depot.

It is really organized in a marvelous fashion, electricity, 220V current, meter, tools laid out in perfect order, shelves on the walls, workbench, welding equipment, etc.

The soldier, who in civilian life worked with locomotives (?), obviously adores his little cubbyhole, which he arranges lovingly and in which he works constantly on piles of repair jobs. He explained everything to me nicely, I expressed admiration for a lot of things, and meant it; he was delighted and I was very interested. I need to cultivate him, to get my bicycle repaired; it's becoming a piece of junk, with tires worn down to the cord.

Dead quiet.

March 7, 1944

Lock forced on the Norman armoire on the third floor.

March 8, 1944

During the night someone staves in the barrel of unstarted cider, probably hoping to find some wine. A lot of cider spilled.

Still, two guards circle the house all night long, and sometimes chatter a little too much under the windows. In these times of terrorists and armed attacks, it gives a reassuring feeling; I sleep like lead.

Little by little, you get to know the men living in the house and to figure out their characters. Bernice is on the best of terms with them and starts interminable conversations; she, who would find a way to talk to a tree, is in heaven, and her nervous condition has disappeared. I would single out the two cooks, Franz and Willy; the armorer Goula, who is a decent boy; the tailor, who one evening, with great mystery, gave me a gift of a loaf of bread. There is also a Pole who sifts flour, to Bernice's great joy (!). As for the *Spiess*,[4] if you don't see him, you hear him! The drivers called him the Neapolitan singer.

Since the departure of the trucks and cars, there are now nine regimental carriages hidden in the park (the horses at Deforge's), along with nine small Russian wagons. Also an antiaircraft machine-gun carrier. To say nothing of the incessant coming and going of wagons between the cannons and the house, carrying the men's food for each meal and all sorts of other things.

My dogs are putting on weight before my eyes. Franz sends them all the bones that have cooked with the soup vegetables, and there are plenty! In addition, Bernice helps herself copiously from the little barrel used to collect the fatty water and scraps. Not everything goes to the battery's pigs (there are four of them at Deforge's).

March 30, 1944

This morning I hear, from my room, psalms being sung in chorus in the barracks room—that is to say, in the parlor—below. Then preaching, then more hymns, another little sermon—new hymns— it's the pastor, who has come to fulfill his mission. I see him leaving, very dignified, looking the part: French army-type cap, knitted scarf, escorted by soldiers, two of whom carry, naturally, the inevitable carbines.

From time to time the men shoot at the innumerable crows that nest in the park.

Odd conversation in the vegetable garden, in the sunshine, with two secretaries from the office.

April 1, 1944

Great stir around the kitchen in the morning. It's only April Fool exchanges, the inevitable jokes, childish and just alike in both countries (to judge by what I'm seeing). They send the Pole, urgently, to take a very heavy case of ammunition on his bicycle to the cannons, where nobody claims it, of course, and we watch him return with his unwieldy parcel. They hang cutout paper fish on the backs of the kitchen girls.[5] I went by there myself, and I must admit I "fell for it." Franz comes to tell me very seriously that "the *Spiess* wants to talk" to me. Fortunately, I have the good sense not to ask him anything; I simply walk by him. He says nothing to me, but Franz delightedly declares me an April Fool. One amuses oneself as one can. (I learned later that in Germany they joke like this for three days, which may be a bit long!)

No more radio! I deposited it at the town hall, like Maltemps and the others. But now you can hear music on the second floor from the linen room, or rather the *Kommandantur*'s day room, and on the third floor from Franz's room. Those who had radios no longer have them, and those who had none have found some.

April 3, 1944

Up until this time, Périers' trees had not been affected; the disaster began this morning. Bernice woke me by announcing that "they" were cutting trees in the drive and along the road (twenty or so already). I leaped up, armed with the paper from the prefect's office forbidding any cutting. The secretary of the *Kommandantur* was nice enough to listen to me, and after a long telephone call to his commander, he followed me down the drive, talked with the young lieutenant in charge of the forty men, infantry engineers, under his command. Obviously, "my" people had no desire to see their natural camouflage disappear. He was therefore sufficiently insistent, and the lieutenant gave the order not to continue any further in the drive or along the road. That much was saved, at least. But alas, they absolutely had to have trees, and without delay. The massacre therefore continued in the woods. All day long they chopped continually, and all day you could hear the falling of the locusts, the elms and alas, the pretty, graceful birches...that I loved so much!

It's horrible to see. You would think that a bombardment had raged in this spot. Trees lying on the ground—over a hundred already! Others cut but tangled up with their neighbors and resisting with all their branches, as if they refused to go. All of them in full strength, stock in full growth, good and straight, trunks clean and robust, in full vigor. Those are all they're taking, chosen for uniform diameter; they'll leave the old ones and the young ones that are still nothing more than saplings. Happy are the dead who do not see this sad thing!

April 4, 1944

Same work as yesterday; what will be the toll and the extent of the disaster? I don't dare think about it. It will all go away, perhaps! The trees are all destined to be buried half their length deep, in holes that are already being prepared for the purpose, to cut up the large, flat expanses in order to prevent airplanes from landing! And to keep these tree trunks from rotting too quickly—they are obviously expecting a long duration—they peel off the bark to a certain height and singe them with a burner. This operation is being carried out in one of the farm pastures, facing the woods. I couldn't watch for long. It seemed to me that these still-living trees were humans being tortured, and I thought I could feel their suffering. The men I interrupted yesterday morning looked at me half jeering, half snarling. What a crew! This morning the farmer spent his time fighting with them. Everything went away: straw, wood, crates, chickens.

Will we have to suffer this for a long time yet? The plain around us is broad, and if it all has to be bristling with trees stuck into the ground, how many will it take? Thousands. The whole woods will not be enough.

There is a certain restlessness in the command; they scour the whole district, most probably with an eye to future works! What is coming next?

April 8, 1944

Same work in the woods. They are not satisfied with the medium-sized stock, they are taking the saplings. Everything is piled along the road before being burned and loaded on the vehicles. In places, there are already completely open clearings. Many French workers from Blainville and Périers are needed to consummate this disaster. There is talk about using the women to dig the holes. (I think I may well be one of them!)

April 9, 1944 — Easter Sunday

Dead quiet. Nobody is working. Capricious weather: heavy showers, rain and wind, followed by very warm sunshine.

April 11, 1944, Tuesday

Birth of two baby goats, Fanette's kids. What a hectic afternoon! I was by myself, Bernice having gone to Caen with her eldest son. About three o'clock I see that Fanette is beginning to suffer; she bleats, pants, acts unhappy. I let her off her tether and shut her up in her stable, where I go often to watch over her. Around four o'clock, everything starts happening: She's stretched out in a corner, cries piteously, and the little feet start to emerge. I bring straw and am there for the birth of two little kids, completely white, all sticky and weak. I am in the process of rubbing them down with straw and helping them come alive when I see Franz's head framed in the doorway. "Chief would like to see car to buy it." This is just the time! Irritated, I say to him, "Just a moment, Franz," and I continue my rather dirty little job. He disappears, and comes back escorted by the captain, the adjutant, Willy, Robert—I don't know who all—and everybody, leaning over the door, takes an interest in the event, contemplates with joy the two little animals that are beginning to shake themselves; they ask a hundred questions in the usual broken French: "How old is *madame* mama?" "In the '*babies*' is there one *monsieur* and one *madame*?" "They're going to be much cold," etc., etc.

Finally, seeing that the two little animals are alive and healthy, I leave them on their straw, explain that I am going to wash my hands— which is certainly necessary—and to take care of the chore that I've anticipated for several days. I get the keys to the garage. Now everyone is interested in the car. They walk around it as best they can, in the middle of all sorts of equipment hastily piled there, and they ask me another hundred questions of a different sort: how many miles per gallon, how fast, etc. A mechanic replacing Goula, who is on leave, raises the hood and notices certain "damage" to the Delco, no battery, no shutoff switch, etc.... I explain.... The captain seems to want it very badly, and examines tires and car with satisfaction. I close the garage and go back to my two little Mickeys, whom I put out in the sunshine and who rapidly dry off and become adorable, with their uncertain movements. The captain and the *Spiess* spend three quarters of an hour admiring them. My washing and bleaching work hardly progresses at all.

April 12, 1944

The cutting of the trees in the woods is proving to be a disaster! They are cutting everything: big locusts, elms in full vigor, the big firs, everything! Nothing will be left but the thicket, in a disarray and chaos that are wretched to behold!

April 13, 1944

Bad day, horribly depressed; all day long the mechanic busies himself at putting my poor little Rosengart in running condition, and succeeds. (And to think that I had stuffed the gasoline tank with powdered sugar...someone gave me the tip, but it didn't work!) I see her circling around what used to be the lawn, coming and going on the road, clean, shiny like before, when the weather was nice, and I am carried back five years, and I miss it, and my heart is so heavy that I can't keep myself from blubbering, right there in the road. My car prancing by, all spick-and-span and being driven by others, the woods that are disappearing, everything that is disappearing...it's too much for one day, and my courage disappears too.

Toward evening I get myself under control; I devote myself to scrounging a few logs, with Bernice's help, and the work does me good.

The hares, panicked by all these men setting posts in the plain, arrive, panicked, in large numbers around the houses, and are slaughtered by Robert, who has killed four of them today and given them to his girlfriend as presents. It's really a nasty day—perhaps someday this will seem like next to nothing. Let's expect the worst.

April 15, 1944, Saturday

Large-scale maneuvers in the sector. Since morning, invasion of the houses by men in complete battle gear. In a drenching rain, they circle around the house with the horses, the wagons, the cars. They're everywhere. They go into all the rooms to try to find some shelter. Young men, almost children, asleep on their feet, looking exhausted. Crackling of rifles and machine guns.

April 16, 1944

Death of the dog Boulot yesterday. He received a terrible blow, running after a female in the countryside. A brute clubbed him. He tried to get back to the house, in spite of his shattered shoulder, fell down along the [illegible], where Bernice went to get him and fortunately had him destroyed fairly quickly by Franz from the kitchen. I was away. I learned the details from her when I got back today; she was crying, showed me his grave in a clump of bushes. None of this helps relieve my horrible depression.

April 17, 1944

Letter from J.O. about the house. What will become of poor Périers later? Is it worth the trouble for me to keep fighting? The French from the village plunder the woods, all delighted by this disaster. It makes my depression complete.

April 18, 1944

I call police headquarters to lodge a complaint against Merière, who is stealing and who answers me insolently that "all the wood" is his, that "it's the Germans who gave it" to him.

April 20, 1944

Nasty day—police — investigation—etc.

April 21, 1944

The car leaves, still without requisition papers. Tomorrow I shall go to Caen, to the *Feldkommandantur* [field headquarters].

April 23, 1944, *Sunday*

Warm sunshine. First appearance of bare torsos sprawled on the grass.

April 24, 1944

Complained to the *Kommandantur* about the car.

Bourdon is really very pleasant — quite amusing conversations heard in the corridors.

April 25, 1944

Celebration of Hitler's name day, on the twentieth. In honor of the occasion, new ranks and decorations are awarded. The men go for a speech at the cannons and come back delighted. The menu is greatly enhanced, they drink not a little (but they don't talk about anything). That evening, a cannon shot.

Franz is made a corporal. Müller is made an *Unteroffizier* [non-commissioned officer]. Weruca and others, *Obergefreiter* [private first class]. He is delighted to get 1,600 francs a month.

April 27, 1944

First important conversation with the *Spiess*.

April 29, 1944

I return from Caen, where the streets are filled with a feverish activity, which makes you think that "something" is going to happen. On my arrival here I find preparations for departure: field kitchen in front of the house, boxes in the hall, papers burned, things put away, etc. In fact, by starting a few conversations I learn that they will leave "probably" on the first of May, that is to say the day after tomorrow. They are waiting for the order. The men are not happy, nor am I, actually. I was beginning to get used to this group, to get to know them all, and they were becoming pleasant. Everything must begin again. And what will the next ones be like? For of course there will be others. In Mathieu, six hundred of them arrived today, billeted in all the houses! What shall we see in the days to come? I am a little fearful, and very nervous!

April 30, 1944

Now it's official. They are going to leave, and are only awaiting the order by telephone. They will be replaced by a motorized unit! Périers has not yet hosted that branch; the collection will be complete!

They leave, without any enthusiasm, for Merville, where they will have to sleep in tents; for all of those from the office, who had good beds, this does not overwhelm them with joy.

On a path in the park I meet a sad-looking soldier, who obviously wants to talk. About the war, naturally, the ruins, the dead—as if it were our fault—he doesn't say it, though, and I don't know what he really thinks. Annoyed, I snap at him: "The war, always the war. Too bad for you, all you have to do is not obey your Hitler." Terrified, he looks in all directions, as if someone could hear us in this isolated spot, in the middle of the trees. Then, very low, with a finger to his lips, he confides something that is probably risky for him: "I'm not a National Socialist." And he leaves very quickly, worried, or perhaps relieved?

Long conversation this evening with the *Spiess* and Weruca, the latter forcefully demanding colonies.

They speak openly about the landing and say, "So much the better. Soon the war will be over."

Everything seems to indicate that the event cannot be far off. Airplanes go over continually, in imposing squadrons. [illegible] today, there is one alert after another, the road is furrowed by transports of all sorts. Today saw Riva Bella after this week's bombardment: impressive damage.

May 1, 1944

The preparations continue. Everything is buckled into sacks, the boxes are ready; they take down the maps and photos tacked to the walls or the armoire doors. French gas-generating trucks and regimental carts begin transporting the ammunition by way of Merville.

None hide their disappointment. You don't hear anything but "*Grand malheur!*"[6] and they are almost emotional. One feels that they are going to make the preparations last as long as possible. They will be replaced by "assault tanks," a large number of which are already quartered at Mathieu!

This evening I attend to their [animals], which are starving and filthy; I try to convince the tailor that out of compassion he should make them "*kaput*" tomorrow. He promises.

May 2, 1944

Quiet day. Ammunition continues to disappear for Gonneville-Merville. After dinner, sitting on the stone from the pond, indescribable conversation with Franz, Willy, and the cobbler.

May 3, 1944

Preparations are taking a new turn; they are emptying the kitchen's reserves, the supplies of canned food, Goula's equipment. In the evening, coming and going of new cars belonging to the area's new units. Nineteen-year-old kids, one of whom is a priest. A moonlit night. Today A.A.[7] at Caen and Lébisey. Death of Brière![8] The traitor known and feared by all.

May 4, 1944

Catastrophic day, which was preceded by a sleepless night because of the incessant noise of cars, trucks, tracked vehicles, coming in and going out continually. Up early. I see the preparations for departure speed up briskly while the new men arrive. And once more there is the laborious, difficult installation of edgy, tired men, who have been traveling for two days and two nights without sleep, coming from Brittany. There are a lot of them — and since they are motorized, they have a lot of trucks, small tracked vehicles, and cars. All these machines move into the park on the cyclamens, hiding under the trees, damaging the young stock. In the drive ten other big trucks artfully lose themselves in the thicket, with what I must admit is consummate skill. You can pass ten paces from them without suspecting a thing, unless the men's voices give them away.

But a lot of men have to be lodged in the house, *Kommandantur* on the second floor, tailor and cobbler on the third—the same old story.

They are a long way from having the equipment that the last ones had, and there are endless requests: a glass, tables, chairs, lamps, etc.—there was even a question at one point of emptying an armoire in the linen room! I avoid this first catastrophe. Noon arrives with a bewildering hubbub of men going up, coming down, nailing, carrying furniture from one room to the other as it suits them. I see the big table from the dining room going up to the second floor, six men carrying it briskly in spite of its weight.

After lunch I come close to total disaster. Doesn't the *Spiess* (very pleased with himself) discover the closed study, full to bursting with furniture, cooking utensils, books, porcelains—everything that I had moved there — and doesn't he have the nerve to want me to move it all to the coachman's rooms in the outbuildings, in order to transform the study into a canteen?! I was insane, desperate, and Bernice was crying! He insisted firmly—I felt that he would not give up — and at the moment when I thought I was lost, I was saved by a warrant officer, speaking remarkable French (two years in the Afrika[9]), extremely nice and understanding. He felt my distress, and whether out of pity, innate courtesy, or understanding of the beauty of the furniture and books—or something else entirely—he intervened, in a private conversation with this terrible *Spiess*, and the dreadful project was suddenly abandoned. When I thanked him later, he said a few very tactful words about the sadness of these damaged houses!

It's so extraordinary that on this day an unexpected and benevolent assistance should appear.

Until evening, continuation of this arduous installation. The mattresses from the big beds disappear into the outbuildings, etc. But one can see that as a group they are under control, well managed, very good discipline, interesting N.C.O.s. Quite a big difference from the previous ones.

Actually, I don't detest all of these men in the same way. There are two levels: When I see coming toward me officers full of arrogance, self-satisfied, probably cruel, my hair stands on end! The enlisted men, the N.C.O.s, the lower they are on the social ladder, the more you can look at them without hate. Apart from a few fanatics, they are simply men like so many others. They are afraid, they are controlled like sheep or like tools, they are often childish, sometimes stupid. Actually, like me they are *unhappy* (for reasons different from mine).

And when they show me their family photos!! Well, then they cry.

Cooking and supply are still here, with their field kitchen, and seem not to be able to decide to leave. Plan, in any case, to return in two weeks, when the motorized unit leaves, and they—supposedly—shouldn't be staying long. But who knows?

And what events may come to pass between now and then! The tiny village of Périers goes to sleep tonight with 220 foreign men. Who could have foreseen that a short time ago? I am exhausted and broken, as after an illness. What a life, what a fight! And always alone...

May 5, 1944

Apparently, they are not supposed to stay more than two weeks. It's certainly a lot of trouble to change everything, upset everything, for such a short time! But *c'est la guerre*, as they say all the time. While going to the mayor's this morning, I learn that the last ones swiped from me, on the morning of their departure, some "silver goblets," probably from one of the armoires in the dining room, where I had found locks broken. It needs to be cleared up, but I can't do it at the moment—the new ones having blocked the furniture with mountains of bread and supplies piled up in cases. I wonder at the habitual "slickness" of the kitchen women, who, having witnessed (?) the theft, thought it a good idea to spread the word through the district, but didn't find a discreet way to tell me at once. It is at least fishy, but what do you expect from such sluts? The day goes by, slow and annoying. Incessant noise of engines, each truck going in its turn to be washed in the courtyard of the farm. All these men are much more "soldiers" than the previous ones: good clicking salutes to the brass! Lectures three times a day by their superiors, demonstration of military steps, shouts, arguments, commotion; it's a barracks, all right!

May 6, 1944

The former dairy currently serves as a shelter for a young pig, rather skinny, who grunts with sincerity.

Bernice spends her time boiling milk and cooking eggs, supplements to a rather reduced ration (she doesn't forget to have some herself).

May 7, 1944

Sunday, nothing special. Various conversations.

Three times a day, muster, inspection, rifle drill, heels clicking, etc.

May 8, 1944

Morning quiet. Afternoon disturbed by an incident that may turn out badly for certain men in the village — an insulting inscription on the dwelling of two women could lead to the arrest of hostages.

The men eighteen to fifty years old dig holes for the posts. This evening (like every evening), with more pomp, helmets, etc., they conduct an inspection of the nine men who will be on patrol all night (three men at a time, relieved every three hours). The night is slow in coming, and from my window I see two of them who pace the drive regularly, while the third makes a circuit around the house and in the park. Unforeseen, strange spectacle for this house of times gone by. Last night there was a full moon. The garden was bathed in brightness, and I saw this man, motionless and helmeted, keeping watch — at the noise of my interior shutters, he jumped, took a few steps in the direction of my room, and watched my window for a very long time — what a strange feeling! A gesture, a posture that he didn't understand, and I would probably go to join those who once lived here so peacefully!

May 9, 1944

They continue to ask me for all sorts of things: lamps, furniture, etc. During the night, huge racket of A.A., bombs, sky lit up by flares, all quite spectacular. The fact of being in bad physical and mental condition makes the nerves more sensitive to all these things, and I shiver for several hours. My folding bed goes "to the guns"—"for the captain." I don't imagine that I shall see it again.

May 10, 1944

According to the latest information, a large number of bombs fell last night (they say two hundred). What I took for A.A. was really bombs. Two that fell in the woods bordering me made enormous craters; we're in a good position to not miss out on our share.

The most striking thing is that the division that just spent two and a half months here and that left for Merville was spotted there because of its battery and was hit! They say one dead and six wounded, among them the tailor and the cobbler! We will have more news soon. Let's hope that it doesn't happen again tonight.

May 11, 1944
Fairly quiet day—a squadron of three hundred passed over! Conversations with the warrant officer who saved me the first day. He is really very nice (eighteen months in Russia, Stalingrad, Moscow—two years in the Afrika).

May 12, 1944
At eleven o'clock in the morning, big film showing, in the stable at the farm; armed sentries at the entrance to the stable and the entrance to the cinema, which means that we are not invited...subject of the film: "espionage"...Night maneuvers, sleep disturbed by the noise.

May 13, 1944
The men are feverishly preparing for the inspection that a colonel is to conduct on Monday; they are very preoccupied with it, and busy themselves around their trucks. All the engines are checked, everything is cleaned, polished, washed. All the vehicles are repainted with a spray gun. Tools are checked and polished. They are worn out with fatigue, and underfed. In the evening there is an unbroken line of men bringing Bernice milk and eggs to cook. If they didn't get a supplement it would be pretty skimpy; one wonders how they can do this amount of work and eat so little.

May 14, 1944
Although it's Sunday, the men continue to work feverishly. They oil cartridges, they continue to put on and take off wheels, they remove the tiniest speck of mud from the patterns on the tires. Right

down to the tailor, who stitches continually. I wonder how they'll be ready tomorrow! I have never seen a unit work so hard. What a difference from the last ones, who idled away the whole day! What a gang of slackers that was! And what drunkards!! These never drink; I even wonder what they take in for liquid during the day. It's a mystery! I never see them with either a mug or a bottle. I see only each evening's milk.

May 15, 1944

The inspection went off without incident. The colonel, who is ill, didn't come, and the captain who replaced him was not, I think, very important. A lot of effort expended for nothing. This afternoon the men were doubtless given a break, which was not undeserved, and you could see all of them asleep on the grass. This evening the house is as quiet as a convent; they're worn out with fatigue.

They're starting to dig holes in the drive, probably foxholes. This house is taking on a more and more deplorable appearance; I'm nauseated, dazed. I'm incapable of the least bit of serious work. I'd like to sleep all day!

May 16, 1944

Unexpected and unforgettable evening! In the kitchen at the farm three men, sitting at a table before three glasses of cognac, sang for hours, for their own pleasure and, without a doubt, for mine. Voices in tune, warm, three different registers and marvelously balanced. They went through everything from "I Had a Kamarad" to the "Merry Widow," the "Beautiful Blue Danube," and their national and popular songs. What a gift those men have! And what sweetness, what engaging nostalgia, what expressive nuances. I could have listened to them all night, and I think that they would have continued without tiring. For the first time I came back in at eleven-fifteen, past an

impassive sentry. Strange evening. On a Normandy farm, three for-
eigners creating a marvelous spell! How bizarre life is!

May 17, 1944

Today they're digging foxholes to shelter themselves from future
bombardments. To begin with, three in what used to be the lawn in
front of the house. A little youngster thought it a good idea to start
one in what is left of the rose bushes; another is under way behind
the houses. This is only the beginning, I think. The men seemed to
be having fun, each displaying his ingenuity for his little personal
underground spot: covering of planks or corrugated metal, clumps
of turf for camouflage, and inside a kind of seat dug out as well as
possible. I laughed to see them working; before, I would have wept
to see this new damage, but now…

The nice warrant officer who saved me the first day is a Protestant…that explains everything! All the men are acquainted with my
pedigree and my husband's life!![10] How strange! They have an intelligence service!

Later: New bombardment of Merville; the house creaks so much
that I can't stay there, and I go down into the garden; I run across
the N.C.O.s in the darkness in front of the stoop. Each man is in his
foxhole.

During the first bombardment my "veterans" were severely shaken
up, one man dead, some wounded, horses killed, and the captain of
the 3rd battery killed! They must have been scared stiff!

May 18, 1944, Ascension Day

Fifteen or so new foxholes have been dug at top speed. They're
everywhere: in the paths, under the thornbush, behind the house,
in the farmyard…this complements the already existing disarray!
And since the men have been ordered to make a roof of earth, to

support that earth they use anything that they can find, so useful planks, indispensable posts, wheelbarrow panels disappear!! Lovely! The sentries who patrol sometimes wear a cap, sometimes a helmet. These last few evenings they have, in addition to a rifle held under the arm ready to fire, a hand grenade stuck in their belt...that's so much more cheery!

May 19, 1944

I spent the morning fighting with men who were taking the doors of the outbuildings to cover their foxholes. I ran down the drive to catch two giants who were carrying one away on their shoulders. Amazingly enough, they were as docile as lambs; I was expecting a humiliating defeat, and I watched dumbfounded as my doors were returned to their places by slightly embarrassed soldiers. I should mention that I threatened one of them with an *offizier*, which always works.

Housekeeping duty: They sweep listlessly, raising clouds of dust, and put the piles of dirt right where you can see them. It's the barracks in all its beauty!

May 20, 1944

Conversation. (Strange man, the *Spiess*!)

May 21, 1944

Arrival in Périers of a new unit, cavalry this time, coming from Plumetot and Cresserons. The numerous horses, the truckloads of fodder, the equipment — without asking anyone, some men take over the pasture along the woods. Just what we needed! We will no longer be able to put the cows there, and what will become of the apple trees? I cut off the water.

May 22, 1944

These horsemen are going to occupy the old farm as well; the rest (field kitchen and so on) is set up at the Le Monde house. Once again there are more soldiers than inhabitants in the village.

May 24, 1944

Ever since the arrival of this motorized unit, on the fourth, there have always been three men on patrol (two in the drive, one circling the house); today they have added one in the garden, which makes four men on sentry duty. The evening inspection of the guards is becoming impressive...thirteen men, including the sergeant!

May 25, 1944

Since this morning, a sentry at the gate, all day long; that's rich! I asked, "*Warum?*" [Why?] and was told, "Order from the chief." That means everything and explains nothing. Let's not press it...

Since yesterday, the electricity is turned off; soon, when the tank is empty, no more water! The motor has stopped! The situation is becoming lovely. Next Tuesday there will be no more gas in town—the situation isn't getting any better.

May 26, 1944

Bernice has a tenant in her house: an N.C.O. who is part of the unit and arrived only today. (Death's heads on his collar.) This presence, combined with the long days of this appalling war, her health, her husband a prisoner, all that makes her frightfully high-strung. In addition, an airplane making a strafing run machine-gunned the house and farm emplacement, as well as the woods, and all this swarm of men, and she was very scared!

May 27, 1944

Conversation with the new arrival (Nana), who is looking forward to cutting the Tommies'[11] throats and will not forgive them their bombardments of Germany. During the night, bombardment. I get into the trench with Bernice. There we meet two soldiers. It wasn't cold, and one feels much more secure than in the house, which shakes from top to bottom.

May 28, 1944, Sunday of Pentecost

Long break for the men, and since it's very warm, there's a big display of half-naked men sprawled on the grass. They have cut some flowers and ask for vases to put them in.

This evening they are all more or less drunk, including *Spiess*, who sings and talks! On the second-floor landing, an unexpected and pleasant evening: an interesting conversation on politics. Night without sleep, airplanes.

May 29, 1944

Monday of Pentecost, bright, drenched in sunshine! Everything radiates the joy of living, peace. The pink thornbush spreads its perfume, the kids and their mother, overwhelmed by the heat, are stretched out in a white heap on the grass. And for the first time I see men really at rest — apart from the obligatory patrol. They loaf around bare-chested or in their underwear, they tease each other, they sleep, and for the first time I see them play cards. Everything is idyllic, everything radiates peace…and yet the sirens have already howled several times, the never-ending airplanes pass over in tight layers, and perhaps this day will be the last! What a contrast and what thoughts! War! All have had enough of it, all look forward enthusiastically to the day when they will return to their homes, most of them are gentle men, dreamers, all of them long for the end, and feel powerless. Today they are all gaiety and blissful relaxation; tomorrow, helmeted and carrying machine guns, they may be Death passing!

Warm evening, perfumed by the pink thornbush, which, in spite of all the insults it has suffered, is an immense bouquet. The men were even drunker than yesterday. Two young men amused the gallery for a long time, holding each other up with great difficulty, hanging on to everything and everybody, bawling, rolling in the dust and, like all drunks, telling mysterious secrets. The N.C.O.s watched them indulgently; they can't act too stern about this, and besides, it's a holiday!

Very late in the night I spoke with the *Spiess,* who was confident, relaxed, and certainly happy to have this conversation. I think that at first he was slightly embarrassed by his tipsiness yesterday. We drew parallels between the German character and the French temperament. He understands a lot of things and inquires passionately about everything. Subtle mind, understanding, mocking, or rather ironic, sensitive to emotion. He leaves tomorrow for four days in Brittany.

The men, having made a counterfeit key to open the transformer, have gotten the electric current back on. That's extremely nice, the motor is running again.

May 30, 1944

Quiet day. We are definitely becoming a sort of "night sanctuary." Each evening, passing troops stop to make a temporary camp and hide under the apple trees in the pasture or under the trees along the drive. They spend the night, milk the cows, pillage a little, sleep, and leave again in the morning. This evening there was a motorized unit, tanks and others, led by a non-commissioned officer who spoke remarkable French and made amusing observations.

May 31, 1944

Quiet day, nothing special, except for an unpleasant birthday. What will the coming year be like? I am beginning it fairly well, in good spirits, but a year is a lot of days when so many things can happen!

Let us hope, and let us try to live without thinking too much. One is not certain of living long at the moment; I would still like to see how all this ends up...

Today the passing troops that hide here are on horse-drawn carriages.

June 1, 1944

Bombardments of Ouistreham—Riva—Besuy—Colleville. We get into the trenches and lie flat on our faces. Pointless to swagger. You aren't at all proud—you're always prepared to get "into the swing of things"! The nights are fairly quiet; the excitement at the moment is in the daytime.

June 3, 1944

German mass in the Périers church. The soldiers mention it to Bernice, who is very proud to clean, to put out flowers, and—the only foreigner—to attend mass, to confess and take communion. Great enthusiasm for the German soldier-priest who hears her confession: He understands only German. "It's real convenient," she says. "You can tell him everything without being embarrassed, and he gives absolution on trust..." "But is it valid, Bernice? Since he doesn't understand anything?" "Of course, madame. He gave me absolution." Oh, I see! It really doesn't matter at all—

June 4, 1944

Quiet, warm day; night, by contrast, filled with the noise of six drunks staggering and bawling. The three N.C.O.s and the "mean *Spiess*" were dead drunk! They click heels nevertheless.

June 6, 1944
Landing!!

During the night of the fifth to the sixth, I am awakened by a considerable rumbling of airplanes and by cannon fire, prolonged but fairly far away. Then noises in the garden and in the house: talking, loading ammunition boxes, nailing. I get up, go to the window. I see the big fifteen-ton truck arriving, coming from the drive and pulling up in front of the stoop, and another truck backing up to the dining room window. I gather that a departure has begun, and I envision the unit moving to a new camp, and in the middle of the night as always. I'm annoyed at the idea of changing troops. I stay up, wondering. I watch through the keyhole of my door, which faces that of the *Kommandantur*. In the light, I catch sight of shadows moving in the office. They're dragging sacks, boxes; they come up and go down. I recognize Mr. George, the bookkeeper, the *Spiess*. They don't look happy. I stay by the window. The airplanes fly over in tight formations, round and round continuously. I envision German airplanes overflying the departure. I'm surprised. But the cannon fire gets closer, intensifies, pounds methodically; what's going on? Great turmoil in the garden. The men have shouted, "Alarm," from man to man, but the siren hasn't sounded. The *Spiess* fidgets, plays with the dog, with his usual air of a man playing at being important...nothing more.

Little by little the gray dawn comes up, but this time around, from the intensity of the aircraft and the cannon an idea springs to mind: landing! I get dressed hurriedly. I cross the garden, the men recognize me. In one of the foxholes in front of the house, I recognize one of the young men from the office; he has headphones on his ears, the telephone having been moved there. Airplanes, cannon right on the coast, almost on us. I cross the road, run to the farm, come across Maltemps. "Well!" I say, "Is this it, this time?" "Yes," he says, "I think so, and I'm really afraid we're in a sector that's being attacked; that's going to be something!" We're deafened by the airplanes, which make a never-ending round, very low; obviously what I thought were German airplanes are quite simply English ones, protecting the landing. Coming from the sea, a dense artificial cloud; it's ominous and begins to be alarming; the first shells hiss over our heads. I feel cold; I'm agitated. I go back home, dress more warmly, close the doors; I go get Bernice to get into the trench, a quick bowl of milk, and we run—just in time! The shells hiss and explode continually. In the trench in the farmyard (the one that was dug in 1940) we find three or four Germans: Leo the cook, his helper, and two others, crouching, not proud (except for Leo, who stays outside to watch). We ask them, "Tommy come?" They say yes, with conviction. Morning in the trench, with overhead the hisses and whines that make you bend even lower. For fun Leo fires a rifle shot at a low-flying airplane, but the *Spiess* appears and chews him out horribly; this is not the time to attract attention. Shells are exploding everywhere, and not far away, with short moments of calm; we take advantage of these to run and deal with the animals, and we return with hearts pounding to burrow into the trench. Each time a shell hisses by too low, I cling to the back of the cook's helper; it makes me feel a little more secure, and he turns around with a vague smile. The fact is that we're all afraid.

Around eleven o'clock, during a lull, I go back to the farm. They show me fifteen or so impact points in the back pasture, impact points on the side toward the church as well, broken branches. We pick up pieces of the missiles, big shell fragments. Mr. George and the replacement *Spiess* come to talk with us; we watch the heavy artificial cloud over the sea being driven by the wind, and especially some balloons in the shape of dirigibles, whose purpose we don't understand. We look at them through field glasses. The Germans talk about the landing, but without nervousness, as if speaking of something that hasn't reached us yet; they look at the collected fragments with interest and smile at us as usual. When someone says to them, "You leave?" they answer, "No, not leave." We don't know what to think; probably they don't either.

One of their men is wounded in the knee. He was in one of the trucks parked on the road across from the church; two comrades lend support, and they take him away in a small car.

Around noon a bit of a lull. We leave to try to have lunch; I busy myself with the fire, Bernice with the soup and potatoes; it's cooking. We start to seat ourselves around the table, two mouthfuls of soup, and then everything changes with tremendous speed. Someone — a Frenchman on the road, the soldiers at the gate — someone said: "The Tommies!" We watch the soldiers. They hide on both sides of the gate, watching in the distance in panic, confusion painted on their faces. And suddenly we hear these words: "The tanks!" A first burst of tracer bullets, very red, sweeps the gate; the men crouch down. Bernice and I hide in a corner of the room. There's banging in every direction. We're going to have to go somewhere else. Standing in our corner, we gulp a plate of soup, while the *Spiess*, who has been shouting orders, comes with revolver in hand to see whether men are hiding with us. Everything starts happening. Evidently, they're going to try to leave with their trucks. A German tank arrives and takes the *Spiess* away. The shells bang.

The mean *Spiess* had guts. He came and went heedless of the shells, attended to everything — and he probably took responsibility for having the trucks leave; orders from higher up didn't seem to come.

Impossible to stay in this house at the edge of the road with such thin walls. We cut two slices of bread, the same amount of cold meat, and hugging the walls of the outbuildings, we make it to the trench, we fall in, and just in time! There's hissing and banging everywhere, our stomachs are churning, we feel suffocated, there's a smell of gunpowder. We stretch out completely, lying on the straw at the far end.

The afternoon is endless. At one point the sound of footsteps makes us jump up and look toward the opening, expecting anything. Consternation: It's the replacement *Spiess* (the nice dark-haired one), who, with a revolver in his hand, his submachine gun under his other arm, and followed by a soldier carrying two boxes of ammunition on his shoulder, has come to see whether there are any stragglers still in the holes. He seems exhausted. He's wounded near the ear and there's a trickle of blood; he sits down for a few moments on the edge of the trench, looking at us with sympathy and as if feeling sorry for us. A few words about his wound, a few words about "the Tommies here," and he leaves. We continue to wait.

The first English soldiers appear in the pasture behind the farm at two o'clock. They come down, submachine guns and machine guns under their arms, walking steadily, not trying to hide at all.

Around six o'clock a lull. We get out and go toward the house to care for the animals and get things to spend the night underground. And then we see the first damage. Branches of the big walnut broken, roof on the outbuildings heavily damaged, a big hole all the way up, a heap of broken roof tiles on the ground, a few windowpanes at my place — hundreds of slates blown off the château, walls cracked, first-floor shutters won't close — but at Bernice's it's worse. An airplane or tank shell (?) has exploded on the paving in her kitchen at the corner of the stairs, and the whole interior of the room is devastated: the big clock, dishes, cooking equipment, walls, everything is riddled with holes, the dishes in broken pieces, as are almost all the windowpanes. The dog Frick that I had shut up in the next room so he wouldn't get killed on the road, is all right and sleeping on a seat. But we realize that if we had stayed there, we would both have been killed. In the face of this certainty, Bernice takes the disaster very well; we try to straighten up the unspeakable mess a little. Out of the question to eat the soup and mashed potatoes that have been prepared; everything is black with dust and full of shards of glass. Someone gives us some soup from the farm. We talk with them for a short while and note that the Germans haven't taken away all the trucks from the drive; there are also a lot of vehicles still in the park.

At the farm, even worse damage. Roof heavily damaged on the hayloft. Jean's room, on the second floor, pierced through by a shell, a beam broken, shell fragments have pulverized his armoire, everything is covered with enough plaster rubble to kill an entire family. Bernadette's room also penetrated, but less so. In the cattle barn a shell has made a very big hole, killed a superb calf, a ewe, and wounded another calf!

In the bedrooms of the farm all the suits, all the clothes are riddled by fragments and unwearable, the hats burned.

In the drive leading to the village, broken trees blocking the way, cut down by the shells, wide breaches in the wall from the passage of the tanks, pillars at the entrance of the old farm on the ground in bits. A cow killed in the pasture.

The English tanks are silhouetted from time to time on the road above Périers. Grand impassioned exchanges on the road with the people from the farm; we are all stupefied by the suddenness of events. I take a few steps down the drive, toward the Deveraux house, and suddenly I see the replacement *Spiess* and his comrade hugging the wall of the pasture. I tell him that he must still have comrades at the guns, since we can still hear the battery firing. You feel that these two men are lost, disoriented, sad. Later, almost night, I see them again, their faces deliberately blackened with charcoal, crossing the park. What will be their fate? How many of them are still in the area, hiding and watching?

Night in the trench, lying on the straw, Bernice and I. It isn't cold. The shells hiss continually over our heads, red streaks in the sky. A few hours of disturbed sleep. Stiff all over.

June 7, 1944

Very early in the morning, German airplane shot down in the field of rapeseed. The aviators (young men) tried to jump with parachutes, but in vain. The bodies are badly damaged, burned, hands still clenched on their parachutes.

Around six o'clock in the morning, dead quiet. We emerge into the coolness of this new day and I go delightedly to stretch out on my bed for a bit. I'm driven from it about eight o'clock by intense cannon fire; we'll spend our time hiding. At ten o'clock I'm wounded.

Above our heads, sudden and horrifying, an airplane battle. I hug the walls of the outbuildings; I'm terrified. I want to get to the trench, to escape these machine gun bullets that smack everywhere. I run; when I get to the turn that leads to the farmyard I throw myself flat on the ground, bewildered, glued to the slope. Suddenly everything's erupting, everything's falling around me, I feel a painful blow to the small of my back. I see balls of fire a few meters in front of me. I raise my head instinctively and catch sight of an airplane falling in flames. All that in a few seconds. I'm mad with terror and distress. I'm talking to myself, I say to myself, "I'm hit," and my first thought is to wonder whether I'll be able to walk. Yes, I can get up, so I walk or run (I don't remember now), and I take refuge, gasping for breath, in the kitchen; I stay on my feet, glued to the wall between the two doors. I lean my head against the wall; I try to calm myself. Blood is running down my face, my left arm hurts, but the right side of my back hurts so much more. So I try to see whether my back is bleeding a lot. I take off my leather belt, and I see that it probably saved me from death, this scout belt bought for the Red Cross and on which I had hung a medallion of St. George. I'm moved in the face of this certain and disturbing fact, that I was protected; by whom? Why? I feel my back; it hurts.

At that moment footsteps around the house. I call. Fortunately it's Bernice, who was afraid and is coming to find shelter. She examines me, tells me that I have a little hole in the small of my back near the spine and that some blood is running out. Evidently, I have a shell fragment, but my legs move, I can walk, and without my belt I would surely be paralyzed! I'm overwhelmed, and so happy to have escaped that! We hear a little less cannon fire. I go up to my room, and there, while washing off the blood and applying a dressing, I take inventory of the damage. Small fragment between the tips of my eyebrows, next to my nose, that won't amount to anything; small hole in my left arm, another fragment that I can probably tolerate for a while. The biggest fragment is certainly the one in the muscle along the spine; we'll see about that one later. My luck is so good that it troubles me. Who protected me??

When we go a moment later with Maltemps to look at the place where I might have died, we realize just what was waiting for me. Major impact points all around the place where I was lying, broken branches, which explains the leaves that I had in my hair, a big shell hole on the little embankment in front of which—at the very second—I should have passed to get to the trench. And the trench itself turned inside out, the metal riddled with holes made by fragments, big impact points all around, airplane debris throughout the farmyard.

The trench will be unusable for tonight, but anyway I've lost all confidence in this illusory safety. Where is safety? Probably nowhere, or in the imponderables that save you.

Day spent hiding, hitting the ground, running. Always the rotten fear, and still at times you get used to it.

House dismal, broken windowpanes, so empty after having been so alive with active men…just since yesterday, what a contrast!

The firing of the naval shells empties you absolutely; you have the feeling that a runaway train is passing over your body.

The straw stacks at the farm catch fire, probably hit by a shell.

The English tanks stream by continually in front of the house; the men salute with two fingers in the shape of a V (victory!?).

French flag hung on the school by the soldiers.

In the evening some excitement: We learn that there are still Germans hidden in the woods. With a boy from the farm leading them, who do we see arriving, drawn, pale, hands dangling, guarded by Tommies with submachine guns? The tailor who slept on the third floor and the tall redhead who constantly worked on his vehicle in the garden. (They were correct and nice.) What a sight: these men surrounded, taken prisoner, sitting on the ground distraught, the little tailor near tears. I'm overwhelmed by this human anguish. I'd like to comfort them, encourage them. I try to get across to them that it's better this way, that for them the war is over, that they won't be killed. The tailor talks to me about his wife, about his child. You sense that he's gripped by anguish, and his eyes constantly seek mine, because he feels that I understand him. We bring them eggs and milk, and we talk with them for a long time; the Tommies are truly accommodating. They both ask to get their overcoats from the cars, and someone escorts them. They come back having found chocolate, and these poor devils who haven't eaten since yesterday want to offer us some. We stay around them until late into the evening. The tailor is very much afraid of sinking on the way to England; he still believes in his country's victory, but not his comrade, who says that they will never have enough equipment to fight. A little later they leave in a truck, waving good-bye to us and somewhat cheered. (There were four of them, two others from the unit in the pasture having been captured too.)

I am horribly sad.

The Périers battery is still defending itself. There are still Germans hiding in the district, many at Mathieu; Le Londel and especially Lébisey are points of heavy resistance.

The Tommies distribute cigarettes, chocolate, candy.

The farmhands, all disreputable types, are very excited and surround them constantly looking for gifts. It isn't pretty.

I'm terribly depressed.

For the night, Bernice and I move into the German bunk beds in the parlor. It's dirty, it's hard, we bang our heads on the upper level getting in. Who could have told me before that I would resort to this? But the trench is wrecked, and the other one, dug behind the toilets, is quite narrow; we would be horribly uncomfortable there for the whole night. We'll jump in if necessary.

Noisy night, cannon fire, airplanes, machine guns, but we're so worn out with fatigue that we sleep a little anyway. Ribs hurt pretty badly in the morning!

June 8, 1944

Still another day like the last. We're still getting shells that kill cows, horses; the animals, terror-stricken, flee everywhere. At the farm we eat the ewe killed in the barn. The Tommies have gotten into the farmers' place and stolen first communion chaplets from their cases, pens, alarm clock, 1,500 francs...

I find that at my house it's the same. My room has been visited. Missing are the pen and two of Maurice's knives, which makes me sad, my big tortoiseshell comb, my silver bracelet, a brooch with a big yellow stone, a pair of lined gloves, leather gloves, a corset belt, three flashlights, which I will miss a lot (a good battery in one of them), and right down to my lipsticks. This is beginning well!! I never saw this kind of thing with the Germans.

Still, the cannon shells hiss. You duck instinctively each time; you get into the holes, you cling to the wall. The park is full of broken branches. You can hear distinctly the orders to the batteries shouted by the commanders. Loudspeaker at each battery, probably, and everything connected by telephone wire.

The English plunder the German vehicles and begin to take them away. The French plunder as well. Nothing but comings and goings in the pasture, in the drive; everyone is carrying something: blankets, clothes, canned goods, often objects of value—field glasses, cameras. Bernice is very excited!

She accumulates everything she can, to the point of wondering what she'll do with all these things. How deplorable it all is! You find all the intimate objects left there by these men in rout: toiletry articles, letters (some never read), photos of women, of children, all of the soldiers' treasures. Some were surprised while shaving and left everything there. They left without overcoats, without underwear, without razors, without food. What a horrible thing is war!! Sadly, I put things away in the office and the bedrooms.

June 9, 1944

Seven o'clock in the morning. Maltemps comes to wake us early, starts chatting by our beds, where we're tossing and turning, so sore. And suddenly, German long-range cannon fire. The house is bracketed by the firing. Probably, they're trying to hit the three tanks located in the hedge of the vegetable garden. We shrivel up in the corners—one can be very thin at times like this! With each shell we hear windows bursting and panes falling. Suddenly there's an explosion at the very door of the parlor, we shrink down even more, feeling death very near. Then we run under the stairs, into the little excavation, where we set up a shelter with German straw pallets. What excitement still!

We're dirty!! Three days without even thinking about washing…will I smell bad? I who was called "the raccoon," making fun of my obsession with washing.

They're looking for Germans roaming and hiding in the district. Englishmen, with revolvers and machine guns in their hands, search the houses. Unfortunately, they start searching in my absence, and since there are locked doors, they find it quite simple to put a bullet in the lock, in my room and on the third floor. In my opinion this is not very conclusive. It smashes the lock permanently but wouldn't stop a man from hiding in the corner; only if he were standing behind the door would he get the bullet in his belly. Besides, they search very badly, in an incomplete fashion.

Naturally, no electricity; wires and poles cut by the shells.

We go to bed without dinner. Maltemps comes to bring us a can of English soup. I'm in pain from the fragment in my back; it bothers me a lot when I walk and makes it horribly difficult to slip quickly into the shelters. My arm is bearable, my eyebrow almost nothing, although there is certainly a fragment buried in each place.

At first light it rains, and all of a sudden there's the sound of glass being crushed below the window, which hasn't a pane left and whose shutters remain wide open. And suddenly, hop! Into the room, jumping through the window, comes a big gray dog; its long hair is wet, it's injured and bleeding, looking lost. A moment of uncertainty; we wonder whether it's going to attack us. It wanders for a moment. I decide to get out of bed to put it outside. But it won't leave us. Whose is it and where did it come from?

The tanks arrive every evening and camp in the pasture of the old farm, whose pillars are down, wide breaches in the walls.

June 10, 1944, Saturday

We are becoming the first camp for the troops coming down from the sea with each arrival of the boats.

A camp is being set up under the apple trees. They're digging trenches, they're setting up tents, they're camouflaging the trucks. It's very lively, picturesque, without any appearance of discipline, no visible brass — or very few, very young lieutenants. No salutes, absolutely no military attitude, no supervision; everyone wanders around as he likes. What a difference from the other army, the German one! There's an uninterrupted stream of people in the house, all of them looking for "souvenirs," or just for things to steal.

It's incredible, all the German equipment abandoned in this hurried flight. The trucks in the drive are crammed with clothes, shoes, blankets, tools, food that was part of the emergency supplies and not taken away! Everyone loots, and it's an incredible mess.

As for the English, they plunder idiotically, destroy a Citroën in good condition with machine gun fire, break the headlights, carry off piles of things only to throw them just anywhere a moment later. I caught one who had been rummaging in the sideboard, which had been inadvertently left open. He had upset everything and was slipping out with a kilo of sugar under his arm. I lecture him and make him give it back. Each time this happens, I make them understand that the *Boche*[12] [Germans] didn't act that way.

Maltemps extracts the shell fragment that I had in the muscle along my spine. I couldn't stand it any longer — it hurt too much with each movement; to lie down at night or fall into the shelters was torture. Picturesque operation on the second floor, in my room, not too close to the window, because of possible explosions. Minimum of antiseptics. A surgical knife, a pair of forceps, a cannula, ether. I told him to imagine that he was operating on one of his horses. It wasn't easy! He was afraid of hurting me (which was true, as far as that goes). He cleaned out the hole, which was full of clothing debris and pus that was beginning to form. I indicated to him what was necessary. He spread the wound open, dug, felt the fragment, pulled on it until it came out. Oof! Rather big fragment, with sharp, jagged edges. Cleaning done with pieces of gauze, which he inserted after carefully rolling them between his thumb and index finger! Even though he didn't wash his hands before, that's pretty good asepsis! But I'm sure that it will go very well, and in spite of the burning, I'm delighted to be rid of it. He's very proud of his exploit and talks about it all day to everyone.

Burial, at the end of the pasture, of three Germans and four Englishmen. Simple, moving, the men with a natural attitude, moved, human, nothing of the German military rigidity. The pastor says the prayers and throws earth on each body as he prays. No military commands, no firing a volley like with the others. It's not conventional; it's human.

Among these troops that camp here in the evening there are some pretty alarming fellows! The shock troops are not, evidently, made up of the elite. Big tattoos, shaved heads, nasty characters that look like ex-convicts. It's a little disturbing for two women alone to go to bed in this huge house, with nonexistent windows, with demolished doors. Fortunately the big lost dog that came to us through the window on that gloomy morning at once became accustomed to the house, which she now considers her own, and to us, whom she loves with the charming demonstrativeness of a young and playful animal. She's docile and has shown herself to be an admirable guard dog, barking (from the first day) when a stranger enters. We make her sleep with us on a German bunk bed, and it's a great security.

Visit to the *Kommandantur*, the office on the second floor, by an Englishman who conducts an examination and searches for interesting papers. He takes away certain things, plus a sample of the iron shell bases left in the drive, which clearly show the scarcity of copper in Germany. He tells me that the "police," or men from the "intelligence service," will come to examine everything and asks me to lock up so that no one can enter.

June 11, 1944, Sunday

We continue to stay dressed night and day ever since the sixth, to wash essential things in haste, to fix our hair on the run. It's very unpleasant and depressing. To be able to wash with hot water, very hot, in one's tub, and go to bed all undressed!! When??

Mass for the English at Mrs. Montblanc's. To think that it's Sunday! A week ago we were lounging or sleeping in the sunshine, in the vegetable garden. The half-naked Germans were spread all around. Bernice played a joke on George the baker by swiping his shoes while he slept. What a change!

We are surrounded by English tanks—twelve in the pasture by the woods, three in the vegetable garden (which is devastated by them and by the German shells that have targeted them), three in the potatoes in the patch beside the drive, an unknown number in the pasture at the old farm, an unknown number on the ridge of the district. An Englishman said: 222 cannons in the district!

More stampedes of panicked or wounded animals, many killed; we bury what we can. It's deplorable, this suffering by the animals, who don't understand anything. The cats are scared and wild, the goat nervous. Poor animals, who suffer the horrible result of the universal folly! I think about them at night! I think about the women, about the children, about the ill who are under this uninterrupted pounding that you hear and that shatters your nerves! What is happening at Caen, still not relieved? I think of all my friends. What do they do; how do they live in that hell? Let me find them alive at least. What do they eat? Here, at least, we are fed as we haven't been for a long time! We eat the animals killed: cows, ewes…and the farm that invites us for lunch every day offers us these enormous, succulent roasts, such as we haven't known for so many years. It's dumbfounding, this situation: cannon, bombs, all the horror of the front and more than copious food, not to mention the chocolate, the cookies, the candy, the innumerable cigarettes, gifts from the English soldiers.

We also have a marvelous pleasure that cheers us as much as this splendid food supply, which is to listen to the radio and be able to follow the course of events. We certainly hadn't counted on it, and we were becoming desperate, the first days, from being isolated, not knowing anything, reduced to conjecture.

But the English camp in the pasture of the old farm has a radio set, connected to storage batteries and set up in the shed on one of the sheaf carts. At the time of each English broadcast, at noon and in the evening, we go to listen; they know us now, leave us alone, and it's the greatest joy of the day.

We learn that the English are following the Caen-Bayeux road toward Isigny and Carentan, probably to cut off the Cotentin.[13]

June 12, 1944

Bad night, with no sleep. Someone comes in the morning to tell us about a mass especially for the French, and said by the English priest in the Montblancs' dining room. Bernice jumps at the idea. I'm tired, under the weather, and I stay. It is in any case prudent to stay at home. Cannons and troops pass through the gate and settle into the garden for the day. Disturbing troops, looters, who are constantly coming into the house, upsetting everything! What a bunch!

In the evening somebody swipes our two mattresses from the sitting room. I find mine a few moments later in the park, on the ground, ready to receive an Englishman for the night. But it's almost dark and I can't look for Bernice's, and then I'm a little bit afraid of verbal abuse. I swipe mine nevertheless, and avoid being seen.

I find a corset belt of mine that was stolen from me. It's incredible. I didn't notice it! It was hanging, all dirty, from one of the gates of the drive. They're crazy! A few moments before, coming back from the rapeseed field where I had gone to see the downed airplane, I found a glove of mine near the hedge!

Radio news of the day:

—Carentan taken, and attempt to join up with the Americans via route no. 13, Cherbourg-Valognes.

—Lison…forest of Cerisy.

—Tilly-sur-Seules, where the fighting is supposed to be very hard.

—Uncertain about the status of the Caen region, which must not have been relieved. Yesterday the Lébisey-Cambes line was still holding.

June 13, 1944

It's cold; my teeth are chattering; I'm scared.

Horrible night. German airplane spotted us and bracketed us with bombs. We are flattened with fear, Bernice and I in the shelter under the stairs. The flashes light us up even there. Even with your eyes closed you "see" this terrible light from the flares. Terrible A.A. The batteries fire at an insane rate. Toward morning a little quiet, but we are broken with fatigue. During the day, soldiers move into the garden and the park, digging in the first shelters, meant for others, made by the Germans. The irony of fate would have it that many of the works made by the first ones will be used by the second ones! And it's a real encampment that emerges, surrounding the house: individual cooking areas, laundry washing, drying on tree branches, tents, foxholes dug everywhere, shouting, singing, etc.; it all swarms with a picturesque and free life that does not in any way resemble the German conception of a camp.

No discipline, no apparent orders given. One notices very few non-commissioned officers, who in any case have no military bearing and don't seem to exert any authority—no salutes, no inspection of arms, or at least none to speak of. Equipment that doesn't look solid, little leather, revolver holsters and cartridge belts made of fabric, torn pockets, scarves made from torn-off scraps of parachute, shoes of every sort, some in pitiful condition. No flashlights, no raincoats, no masks, poorly maintained rifles that they lay just anywhere. If it weren't for the helmets embellished with little camouflage rags and the khaki color of the clothing, one might think it a vast holiday camp!

I think that a man could fling himself into a corner and snooze all day without being bothered. What a change! I can get two placards in English to attach to each side of the house, forbidding entry without an order. I requested them from a distinguished Englishman, aristocratic, who speaks a sort of French; there are a few like him, among so many alarming fellows and so many seedy tattoos. I had an interesting conversation with him and spoke to him about the disorder that we fear from the domestic point of view. He asked me certain questions (about the farmer, mayor); vague answers, of course.

The lost dog, christened Nelle, proves to be adorable.

For the first time today I went all the way to the cemetery. Trucks are stationed in all the hedges leading to it, bordering the pastures. Encampment everywhere, but what is unexpected, in the cemetery itself! Tents, various shelters, underground shelters. The church benches are outside and serving unexpected purposes. As for the church, it's open, laundry drying inside on cords. The statues of the Virgin and of St. Ouen have been taken down from their pedestals and walk around on the floor. Men eat, sleep, and live there!! If anyone had seen the Germans do the same, they would have cried shame and sacrilege!

We go regularly at noon and at seven o'clock to hear the news on the radio.

*Marie-Louise Osmont in the gardens of Château Périers,
where she enjoyed the outdoors and the rural way of life.*

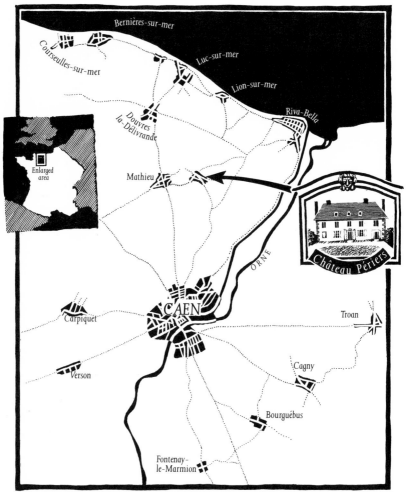

Above: *The countryside surrounding Périers made up the Osmonts'
world. Nearby Caen offered theater and dining, and a bicycle trip to
the coast was a day's jaunt.*
Above right: *Château Périers, home of Marie-Louise Osmont.
About the house she wrote, "From it I get something like a magic spell:
I feel myself in intimate communion with it."*
Right: *Dr. Osmont in his first-floor office at Château Périers.*

PÉRIERS-SUR-LE-DAN — Le Château

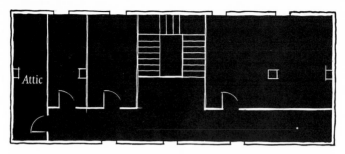

Third floor

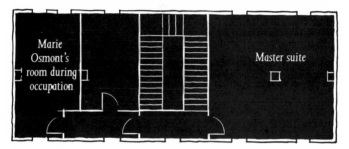

Second

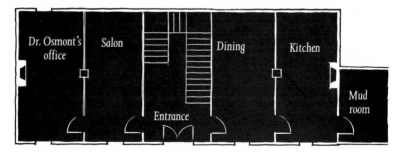

First floor

Floor plans of Château Périers
(not to scale)

Marie-Louise Osmont with her beloved pets. Even during the war, she worried for her animals, and sought great comfort in their company.

The grounds of Château Périers. The narrow buildings to the right of the chateau are stables; farther to the right is a small building for making cheese. Marie-Louise's greenhouse is in the garden behind the chateau.

Bernice and her family lived in the gatehouse at the entrance to the driveway, and the tenant farmers, the Maltemps, lived across the road in the cluster of farm buildings.

Dr. Maurice and Marie-Louise Osmont.

Here is today's:

—Caen still holding, it has been bombed!! Tons of explosives!!

—Line from Bayeux—Tilly-sur-Seules—Balleroy—Carentan—St-Lô.

—Fall of Pont-l'Abbé...Montebourg.

—Bombardment of bridges, railroad stations: Mézidon, Caudebec, Grimbost forest, Tours, etc....

—The German army opposing the advance of the English army is made up of 250,000 men; the English have taken 10,000 prisoners.

—The 4th American Division is operating in the Cotentin.

—The English flotilla fired 16,000 tons of shells during the first days.

—The Belgian king, Leopold, was taken to Germany as a prisoner on June 7, in violation of the assurances of the armistice.

—Churchill has come to Courseulles to see the operations for himself.

June 14, 1944

Night of the thirteenth to fourteenth very bad. The German airplane that came yesterday recommenced its rounds beginning at eleven o'clock. The droning, the nosedives, the silence in which you listen to it (the A.A. batteries don't fire) — it's all horrendous. We're constantly expecting to die. Maltemps didn't want to spend the night under the road bridge with his family and his servants any longer; he came to sleep under the stairs. At the beginning it gave me a feeling of security, I don't know why, but then he irritates me a little — he talks constantly, predicts the worst, and snores like a locomotive. I was quite tired in the morning. The paving is even harder than the wood of the beds, we're cold, and with three of us it's too tight to move. But where to go? Where can one avoid being killed? Terrible bombs fell, and you could hear the slates, the tiles, and the windowpanes falling.

The outbuildings are more and more in ruins, the garden is a disaster, the house is still standing. Everything is disgustingly dirty; there's stuff all over the floor; you walk on all that all day long. Let's hope that the house continues to stand. When it was such a burden on me, I sometimes wished, stupidly, for a bomb to destroy it. Now I want it to be preserved! Strange!

Noon bulletin:

—Capture of Caumont near Bayeux, tank battle around Caen—the enemy is resisting and putting pressure on Carentan.

—Capture of Ham near Cherbourg.

We'll see this evening whether it's more detailed.

Still copious meals at the farm.

I slept for two hours this afternoon, stretched out on a real bed—what bliss!

In the evening, interesting conversation with a soldier who explains to us the purpose of the balloons attached to each end of the boats: They are connected by cables, thus preventing airplanes from flying over to bomb.

During the night, the German airplanes again come to drop their bombs; I'm calm, but sleepless, sometimes stretched out under the stair vault, sometimes on the bedstead in the parlor. In the morning, terribly stiff.

June 15, 1944, Thursday

The big event of the morning for me was my first hot bath! What a pleasure to be able to get completely undressed, soak in hot water and soap, change all my clothes. It transformed my spirits; it seems to me that everything is going to be all right.

Still, on the noon bulletin nothing very heartening. Caen has not been freed. Very hard tank fighting between Caen and Tilly. Undoubtedly, a lot of airplanes are plastering poor Caen with bombs!

—Le Ham-Carentan English counterattack.

—1,700 km of territory taken by the allies.

—de Gaule in France—[passage blacked out]

A sergeant who sleeps in the park comes to eat with us! We're already beginning to get to know him a little. He's a character! Professional soldier with twenty-four years of service: India, Syria, Africa (Tunisia, Morocco), Iran, Palestine, West and South Africa, Turkey, Spain!! He's philosophical and full of humor. He says with conviction, "*c'est la guerre*," and "*c'est nécessaire*" [it's necessary], with the smile and, naturally, the accent. (It was this "professional" who had me leave the house, one of the first days, because he was going to detonate an unexploded winged bomb behind the house. "Very nasty," as he said. Without any doubt it was one of those that wounded me; from the way he described it to me, I recognized the debris found that day.)

Since he knows that we sleep in the house, he came to familiarize himself with the place in order to "come get you if the house is `broken' on you." It is at the same time comforting and refreshing! Let's hope that...

In the afternoon two Englishmen come to speak to me (the professor and the Welshman, both intelligent, distinguished). I know them already from having spoken with them, the professor with regard to the policing necessary to maintain order. They come to look for "*Boche*" chairs and tables in order to be "*confortable*" [cushy]. We go up to the vegetable garden together to see the motor. During that time somebody swipes two more mattresses from me!! I find one in the grass, which I take back myself (I'm beginning to get practiced at the maneuver), but the other isn't to be found. I shall bring it up with the traveling sergeant and professional soldier.

What thieves these soldiers are! In the vegetable garden they have dug up all the potatoes as big as walnuts. There are no green peas left, no more garlic or shallots. The potato field at the farm is full of men in the process of digging them up! Incessant gifts of chocolate and cigarettes, thefts of other things!

They tell us that England has only one care—to send us abundant provisions as soon as possible. Let's hope so, otherwise this winter we'll starve.

Fairly comfortable night under the stair vault, which I have organized for the better, with several thicknesses of mattresses. I had taken a sleeping pill and I slept like lead from midnight on. Supposedly, the German airplane came back to drop its bombs; I didn't hear a thing! If only all the nights could be like that.

June 16, 1944, Friday

I'm out of sorts. Stormy weather and especially German firing with big pieces; it isn't pleasant.

And especially because of unexciting news on the radio. Situation unchanged at Caen. Advance to the west of Pont-l'Abbé—Carentan must have been lost, since they report that the English guns are shelling it. They talk about Sainte-Mère-Eglise. It seems to be taking so long! And yet on the map it represents a wide front. But it's the Caen question that preoccupies me.

Found some interesting papers in the second-floor office.

The camp in the park and garden settles into its little routines. The shelters are being improved (poor garden, unfortunate cyclamens!), the open-air kitchens proceed in their own way. Each consists of a metal cracker box into which they put dirt, which they douse with gasoline without sparing the precious liquid; and they light it. It reeks all the way to the second floor.

Great difference from the German soldiers: The English seem absolutely free and sing or bawl any old song while they're busy doing something (no comparison with the musicality of the last ones). But at least there is a certain air of happiness about them. It's true that they have barely begun the war and that the others had had more than enough of it!!!

Around seven-thirty, a terrifying hail of bullets above our heads. A German airplane pursued by an English one that is machine-gunning him from above, an American on his flank. A few seconds of terror— you don't know where to hide, it's banging everywhere with a terrifying intensity. Bernice, who was outside, arrives, very pale. The German airplane is shot down 3 km away, another at Blainville (?). Two wounded, one killed in the pasture camp; one of their trucks in flames.

June 17, 1944

Passable night in spite of the eternal German airplanes and their bombs.

Better news on the radio: capture of St-Sauveur-le-Vicomte. The Americans are 7 km from La Haye-du-Puits. The attacks to the east of Caen repulsed. King George has come to the front.

I learn that Caen was bombarded twice during the day on Tuesday the sixth, and throughout the whole city! I am afraid for the people I know, and I also wonder—it's quite a different thing, but nevertheless pretty important—whether the banks' vaults will have held up under the concussion! If not, I am penniless! We shall see!

Day cool at the beginning, then sunny.

Still, military life swarming outside the house. Incessant noise of the trucks and small tracked vehicles, which come and go in an infernal dust.

I must say that they drive infinitely better than the Germans, with smoothness and precision. With everything that is coming in and going out through the gate, with the Germans the pillars would have long ago been on the ground!

The mayor has had our radios given back to us, but no current, probably not for a long time.

On the road, some unfortunate refugees fleeing with their belongings and their child. They're coming from Hérouvillette, where life is no longer possible, which was bombarded and leveled, and they're going on foot all the way to Grandcamps in stages!

9:30 P.M.: Rotten firing of long-range cannon. Coming back from the cemetery, where I went with apprehension in the first place. I flung myself flat on the ground four times. The shells were exploding in the pasture and hissing by at head level. I raced to join Jean and Bernice, who were hiding under the bridge. All the English in their holes, and they were scared! The face of one of them was streaming with sweat...but naturally, once the alert was over, they broke into noisy peals of laughter, except for one, who was trembling like a leaf.

Pretty bad night. Again the German airplane that comes to prowl for hours and drop bombs. At eleven o'clock he dives, drops his flare and boom, drops his bomb very nearby. You hear windowpanes and slates flying; the dog Nelle, in total panic, comes to take refuge with us. The concussion and the blast open all the exterior shutters of the kitchen and the dining room, as well as the doors, which bang. Where there are hooks, the wood of the window frames is ripped out! I have to get up to close what I can, because the cold is coming in on us. Sleep doesn't come until morning, when a violent artillery duel starts up. Shells near the bakery and in the little pasture. For the first time since the beginning, I don't go to listen to the radio at noon. Too many explosions everywhere. I'm tired and sad. Deliverance?? Perhaps death and ruin instead...then what should one wish for? Chaos of ideas! We don't know what to wish for, what to hope for. And what's more: gray, cold weather. And still no hope of seeing Caen again very soon.

June 18, 1944, Sunday

Today cold, so different from what it was like two weeks ago, when we lay toasting in the sun, with Germans taking the sun cure in the grass. What has become of stout George the baker, a decent sort and so little suited for war?!

A shell this morning killed an Englishman in the drive! Since the beginning, four English officers killed. This evening after dinner we watched, behind the farm, a magnificent descent of parachute troops. The big four-engine planes came in rather high, greeted by sustained A.A. But they passed unscathed, then we saw them descend little by little, slow, heavy, and maneuvering with splendid assurance. And suddenly, from an airplane that had come down rather low, there emerged, like a bouquet of flowers, a whole flight of parachutes (of all colors, each color indicating the contents of the container). Each airplane in turn dropped its cargo of white balloons. It was impressive and splendid. The men fell too far away for us to make out their shapes, the point chosen being the fields between Périers and Colleville, but the maneuver was truly beautiful to see, of these immense birds dropping their human cargo. Weather splendid and calm, without any wind.

The English troops have supposedly cut off the Cotentin. I didn't go to listen to the radio. The crowd that comes to listen disgusts me and I'm tired.

Later: Good news regarding the Cotentin, which has been cut off, Cherbourg isolated—this is certainly a hard blow to the Germans.

In our area, fighting at Troarn. A naval gun (the one that was making so much noise yesterday) has silenced a big German piece at Houlgate.

A worker from the farm, who left yesterday by bicycle for Troarn to try to see his family, returned without having been able to get there and with visions of horror on that battlefield: burned tanks, parachutes caught in the trees, gliders, English and German helmets in the road, puddles of blood everywhere!!

The professional sergeant, easygoing and devil-may-care, has become a pal. He joins us when we eat and brings us all sorts of things: canned food, crackers, beautiful empty metal boxes that delight Bernice. What a strange existence!

Ironing, mending, as if we weren't at war…perhaps in a few hours we shall crawl once again into the shelters.

June 19, 1944

Night deliciously quiet. A few explosions at the beginning, then nothing more. When I wake I understand why—a fine rain has set in; I take advantage of it to go sleep a few hours more in my bed, still fully dressed, but it's so nice! Ah! To finally be able to sleep undressed!

You really shiver in the house, with all the windows missing their panes.

Day rainy and breathtakingly silent.

From time to time the batteries let loose, but everything very soon falls silent again. No airplanes. It's very restful for the nerves. Serious and salutary washing up.

The camp continues and perfects its installation around the house; they're digging everywhere. Command post and telephones under the little bridge, beside the abutment. Kitchens everywhere; they're putting a big one in the second garage, whose roof is missing.

Comical thing: the Irish cobbler, a little crazy, insists on resoling some shoes for me; I take him some, and some clogs as well. The clogs are returned a few moments later with magnificent hobnails.

My sergeant told me that two days ago a German from Lébisey arrived at Biéville to give himself up. He said that at the beginning there were 150 men, but that the number decreases every day because of the killed and wounded. Poor morale, provisions running out. And still they hold out.

Radio news for the nineteenth: Carteret-Valognes line — south of Carentan on the Vire Barneville — naval cannon of the Ramili[14] silence Houlgate cannon — account of the capture of the Douvres-la-Délivrande (Bally) *Blockhaus* [blockhouse], which held out for ten days with fifty men.

June 20, 1944, Tuesday

Resumption of the artillery duel, hiss of the German shells answering. Installation at the farm of a large Red Cross station: trucks, tents — granaries and barns taken over by the hospital personnel.

At 5:30 P.M. big airplane battle. Two Germans shot down: one at the head of the road to Lion, the other at Beuville at the crossroads where the well is, in front of the Marin house. Many civilian and English wounded brought by ambulance; one Englishman killed. It must not have been pretty to see. The ammunition exploded at the instant of the crash, and some people from Beuville had gathered at the well. Here, for a long time the leaves of the trees, ripped off by machine-gun bullets, fell around us.

They have announced the arrival (unconfirmed) of a contingent of de Gaulle's army and Americans who are said to be coming to complete the capture of Caen, whose fall is very slow in coming... what condition must the poor city be in? Lébisey is still holding out. American army 8 km from Cherbourg.

Quiet night, with half a sleeping pill. Lots of A.A. — but sleep — and at seven o'clock back to my bed on the second floor.

The English are said to still be searching in Périers for hidden Germans??

The Americans are 5 km from Cherbourg — 2 km from St-Lô — Valogne taken — Les Pieux.

Capture of Ronchy, in Calvados.

June 21, 1944

Gray weather. There is supposedly fighting (?) in the streets of Caen; Rue St-Jean is said to be leveled. (!?)

Conversation with a Red Cross soldier, who speaks French very well. I propose to him that an operating room be set up at the house. He will speak to his colonel about it. Interesting man.

All day, German firing around us; the shells hiss with regularity. A worker at the farm is wounded in the neck and in the foot, in the hay field that they were mowing; a horse wounded and has to be destroyed.

7:30 P.M.—It's banging impressively, and so close! Falling shells, bombs...what a life! And so many others more unfortunate than we! The poor cows behind the farm are terrified and haven't eaten today.

I am starting to do my evening washing up around eight-thirty, when someone calls me. Two Englishmen are waiting for me on the stoop: I recognize the nurse soldier from this morning, who introduces the chaplain to me. And he asks me for permission to say mass (his private mass) tomorrow morning in the house. Place selected: the office on the second floor, which I hasten—after their departure, embellished with endless formalities—to clear of all the Germans' debris (papers, all sorts of rubbish, bottles, etc.). Bernice is delighted and makes bouquets. I put out a white cloth, candles, crucifix, and flowers. But I can't help reflecting and smiling...this house, with such Protestant origins, is going to have mass said within its walls! What a strange thing. With the Germans a few months ago, a Protestant service in the parlor; today Catholic prayers...what shall we see before the end?

June 22, 1944

The mass is for a quarter to eight. I arose quickly, washed up even more quickly, the priest and his server being there ahead of time.

Low mass heard by Mrs. Maltemps, Bernice, and myself. At the end, profuse thanks from the priest, who finds the improvised altar "*beautiful*." The big table from the dining room, decorated with flowers, is in fact rather pretty, in this still-dirty room with its windows broken, its armoire pierced by a bullet.

Coincidence or effect of my getting up quickly, or of the bad night listening to airplanes and bombs: I'm depressed and sleepy all day. I lay down and slept in the afternoon.

It's 6:00 P.M. In a gloriously clear sky blazing with sunshine, formidable squadrons of airplanes pass over. Shining like silver, heavy, slow, and terrible, they are going to sow death...where? I tremble for all those unfortunate French, for Caen perhaps! What a horrible thing!

Violent artillery all day, shells everywhere in Périers, some English gravely wounded, some animals hit. You feel yourself in danger all the time. Around seven o'clock, English squadrons come despite violent A.A., to bomb near Caen (where?), you can see the strings of bombs falling; it's sinister—

This evening a dramatic turn of events: They took Maltemps to Colleville to be interrogated by an English officer. Vague search. Drawers and armoires. The soldiers who took him away said that he wouldn't be back this evening. Mystery. Is this because of a filthy denunciation, revenge by someone in the district? I hope that it will work out all right. His wife is distraught.

Advance continues toward Cherbourg, where there is fighting in the outlying areas—heard the name Ste-Croix-Hague, probably the home country of Aunt Mimi and Mr. Lignoir.

Tilly-sur-Seules is still the scene of impassioned fighting: taken, lost, and retaken endlessly, a soldier tells me that its walls are leveled. Nothing about Caen in the bulletin; according to the same soldiers, the city has been bombed...what a costly and terrible "liberation"!!

Marie-Louise Osmont

June 23, 1944

Night hard to get through with the continuous din of the bombs and the A.A. It's dreadful, and yet for short moments I fall asleep and even into dreams, most often ominous; but still one is all freshness, pink dresses, singing children, airy dances...a brutal cannon shot brings me out of this enchantment. Ah, to see beautiful, fresh, wholesome things again! Music, light ballets...but when?

Mass again on the second floor. I attend alone! Am I becoming pious?

Maltemps will not be back today. His wife made inquiries of an officer here. He is accused of collaboration! He'll be detained several days at Colleville. Between noon and two o'clock, thirty-five shells bracket the house and the farm! Since this morning it's a hell of cannon fire from both sides—English wounded—(in seventeen days, seven or eight officers killed in the sector)—found photos.

This evening large four-engine planes flying low and at reduced speed again drop their flights of paratroops. It's very beautiful.

June 24, 1944

Ordinary night, not too bad. Day of relative safety. On the other hand, Beuville is plastered. Splendid weather, still many balloons over the sea. The camp around the house continues its swarming life and keeps its air of people on vacation, always singing. After lunch, return of Maltemps. Reason for his incarceration? Vague...not formulated. It seems his attitudes are suspect! I think rather of a maneuver by people in the district.

It seems that I am also to be targeted. I am accused of "collaboration" for having, on Wednesday evening June 7, given milk and eggs to the two German prisoners who had just been captured in the woods (the tailor and the tall redhead)! So! Those who accuse me, the mayor and others, found it quite appropriate to sell them, at a very high price, two days earlier, milk, eggs, and butter! But to give out of compassion, out of simple human feeling, something to drink to two disarmed, gaunt, terrified, and famished men, that is a crime! What a mentality!! There are individuals with whom one will never be able to see eye to eye: They are stupid or hateful or malevolent; one doesn't know! Theft and profiteering are allowed, tolerated, and even protected. Plain instinctive compassion is a crime...poor humankind!

Mass again on the second floor.

Satisfactory news from around Cherbourg, where the battle rages for possession of the strongpoints. Advance northeast of Caen, capture of Escoville and Cuverville. My sergeant tells me that a German patrol with cannon was at Château de la Londe yesterday!

June 25, 1944

Very hard night. Airplanes, bombs, shelling of Beuville, some houses destroyed, Mr. Marin killed. I sleep a little nevertheless; you get used to anything!

Mass in the Périers church, cleared of its encampment of Tommies and cleaned. A lot of people from the district, a lot of Englishmen, many of whom take communion. Splendid weather! I think of the picnics of former times...where are those happy days? I would like to go to see the coast by bicycle. I'm torn between a great desire to do it and the fear of a shell! Finally our sergeant advises me against it, as too "*dangerous.*"

At 8 P.M., sad traffic past the house, of unfortunates fleeing Biéville, where the shells rain down, animals all killed or wounded. Vehicles loaded with mattresses and everything that they're trying to save. Gloomy thoughts, for one thinks, egotistically, of oneself!

June 26, 1944

Rain during the night, not too many bombs, still slept badly. This morning, intense shelling by both sides—barrage fire—the noise is maddening!

Around five o'clock in the afternoon it's Bernice who is suddenly seized with a mad desire to go see the coast, and she takes me with her, the sergeant having said that there was not too much danger today. "Good luck," he tells us, and we agree, laughing, that if we're not back at eight o'clock this evening, he'll follow the route by motorcycle to see whether we're dead.

The trip is worth the risk. Troops everywhere in picturesque camps half underground, half in tents, an intense coming and going of trucks, small tracked vehicles, motorcycles. At intersections, policemen with their forearms encased in white sleevecovers indicate whether the way is clear or not. It's an intense, robust, and reassuring bustle of life. Roads have already been built at record speed, the ground covered with strong wire mesh. Plumetot has suffered, but Cresserons even more, the old part of Luc not too much, but all the houses on the seawall, from one end of the shore to the other, have been wrecked. The landing has not left a single one intact, they are gutted, pierced through by shells or bomb fragments. I hope that the inhabitants were able to flee. But the magnificent spectacle is on the sea, where a whole fleet of big ships and smaller boats is anchored. On the horizon all the way to Bernières, an imposing and numberless fleet is deployed, protected by its balloons, but not really concerned about the enemy. One is taken aback by this strength and this air of security. The Germans could certainly never have foreseen such a thing; it's beyond them. Despite the frightful damage, despite the constant presence of Death, you cannot help admiring this audacity and this power. It's beautiful as a dream and alarming as a nightmare. Men are capable of anything, but alas, only to destroy!

On the seawall roll the famous amphibious cars, still all wet from leaving the water, these "ducks" with retractable wheels, a rear propeller, big boats rolling on wheels.

We go on all the way to Hermanville, very hard hit, including the church. We push on as far as the Bost house: heartbreaking spectacle of a house entirely burned, since Tuesday the sixth at seven o'clock, by shells. These poor people have nothing left, staying at a neighboring house and wearing borrowed things. At sixty years old! And after having built and improved their house day after day through their frugality!

We are taken by surprise, on the way back, by a stormy and torrential rain; we stop against a wall. Coincidentally, a car from the 42nd in the pasture stops, recognizes us, and the very amiable officer takes us in, has our two bikes strapped onto the hood, and takes us back all the way inside the gate! Bernice is cheerful. I am delighted with my outing, in spite of seeing those poor Bosts, who will haunt me tonight, and how many others, strangers. In any case I see that it is possible to leave Périers, where I was beginning to suffer from nerves; inaction under the shower of shells is not healthy. (Shell fell a few meters from the gate; many in the road and in the woods.)

We are now perfectly used to the noise of the batteries, though. The "outgoing" that bang so sharply a few meters from us no longer make us jump; we pass without flinching through the volleys of blasts.

The animals have adjusted perfectly to it. In order of adaptation, I think it was the dogs who started, then the birds, the rabbits, the goat, and lastly the cats. The two female cats are still all thin and fearful from it. They mew for no reason.

Rainy night, fairly quiet as far as airplanes. Sustained cannon fire between Caen and us.

Good news yesterday: Cherbourg almost captured.

Russian offensive; Vitebsk taken.

June 27, 1944

In the morning, another mass on the second floor; an officer who comes to attend and to *take communion* finds a way to carry off a metal trunk and upset everything. Protest on my part. If one cannot even be safe with those who come to worship! Well...

After lunch I convince Mrs. Maltemps to visit the coast with me. Plumetot. Cresserons. Lion. La Brèche d'Hermanville. The sea is blue, drenched with sunlight, and it's an unforgettable spectacle, this numberless flotilla moored so close to shore. We watch the ceaseless coming and going of the "ducks" that cut through the water so rapidly, their propellers leaving white swirls; then they arrive calmly onto the sand, rolling on their big tires, they turn smoothly, and take the road of wire mesh that runs along the water. They're loaded with all the equipment, cases of rations, gasoline, etc., that they go to get from on board the great vessels positioned farther out. It's unforgettable! Like an old print recalling the great naval battles, to which are added all the wonders of modern science. For the first time during these three horrendous weeks, I feel an excitement and a sort of barbaric joy to see with my own eyes this phenomenal spectacle of the most horrible and the most modern of wars. From time to time a shell coming from far away explodes near a big ship. Signals by mirror, signals on land; on the seawall, where they let you go in peace, there's a coming and going of tall, laughing youngsters, who all bid you good day. (Since leaving Périers we have responded over one hundred times to these friendly greetings.)

The LaRues' house demolished and unrepairable; there are nothing but ruins in that whole area, and the great villas of La Brèche are charred stumps. All these houses along the edge are no longer anything but ominous, gutted, demolished remains!!

Incredible traffic on the roads, and at La Délivrande the police-man-soldiers with the white arms have a lot to do to direct the masses moving in every direction…a Place de l'Opéra with trucks, small tracked vehicles, "ducks," and men in khaki. It's truly strange. This outing did me enormous good.

Saw for the first time at La Délivrande: leaving a large tent camp, English Red Cross women. Dressed exactly like soldiers—long khaki trousers. I envy them for being young and being able to make themselves useful. My inaction weighs on me. The organized ambulance units have no need of the French, and not knowing English is a great inconvenience.

Cherbourg captured. Below Caen, Cheux and Fontenay captured.(?) Violent shelling all day.

They are still fighting very nearby. Sprays from the shells falling on Mathieu, Le Londel. Machine guns very close. We have been right at the front for *three weeks* today. So when will Caen be taken? When will we have a little quiet? When will poor France be finished with all her misery and all her sorrows? Ah, to rediscover peace, courage, and to rebuild everything: Château Périers, which was so dear to Maurice, and our unfortunate France, which has so much to do in order to rise again.

Let us hope!

June 28, 1944

Cannon all night, artillery duel, raging A.A., an infernal noise! Cannon all day!! When will it ever cease? From time to time, in the short silences, you hear the refreshing song of the few birds remaining in the park. The trees are losing all the leaves from their crowns; the wind from the shells plucks them. It's summer, sometimes one is almost cold, then it becomes stormy, but never truly fine weather.

Butterfly bombs (the same as the one that wounded me) fell at two o'clock in the farmyard, very near the goat. What noise! It's stupefying!

Bulletin: American engineers are reorganizing Cherbourg's highways, strongpoints, and communications. (German general and admiral taken prisoner.) Southwest of Caen, Cheux taken, Tourville; the road from Villers-Bocage to Caen has been cut. There are twelve German divisions in the Caen sector!

During the evening, long conversation with the stretcher-bearer, so proud of his "British empire." He nevertheless has an open mind; he's very cultured, and it's interesting to exchange philosophical ideas with him.

June 29, 1944

Good night, fairly quiet. This morning the cannons finally fell completely silent; probably, the last fourty-eight hours have been preparation for this furious battle that you can hear toward Caen. The cannon's terrible voice has given way to the terrible hand-to-hand that one imagines!!

Crossing of the Odon.

Advance to the southeast of Caen, toward Evrecy, 4 km from the Orne. Weakening of local resistance to the northeast of Caen (probably yesterday's fight at the Château de la Londe, so close to us). A movement to encircle Caen is taking shape.

A sensational feat for me: For the first time I am beginning to clean up the horrible dirt and disorder left by the fleeing Germans. I began, without knowing why, in the dining room. Until now I have had neither the strength nor the desire to undertake any work of this sort. I was living in a semi-brutishness caused by this noise, by this unbelievable and dangerous life right at the front. I was waiting...everything seemed pointless to me, in the face of this constant peril. Today for the first time I was motivated by one of those forces that often drive me without my will having anything to do with it. From this first effort—so small in the face of the immense task—I feel a lightening of my burden. Perhaps I will put this house back on its feet; who knows? This house that has been by turns my despair, my worry, my refuge, and perhaps my only security. From it I get something like a magic spell: I feel myself in intimate communion with it. What powers could these old stones have, what secret energy could have been left by the departed who once lived here? Will I be able, here, to regain peace and the will to live through the troubling days to come? To create in this topsy-turvy universe a spot, however small, of peace, harmony, beauty? Will I be able to put it all back on its feet before I go to sleep forever? (Forlorn hope!)

June 30, 1944

What a plastering today! The shells hiss and fall continually in the pasture behind the farm. Two cows killed, one wounded…poor beasts! I'm so depressed!! Cleaned the parlor and demolished the seven German two-level bunk beds. This evening the four-engine planes came to drop their paratroops.

Rotten night; intense cannon fire, an uninterrupted rumbling that shakes the ground and the house!

Situation unchanged to the southwest of Caen. How long it's taking. The magnificent church at Vorrey destroyed…what butchery. They announce 92,000 men taken prisoner in Normandy; 121 tanks completely destroyed; 171 out of commission…they don't talk about the civilians!

July 1, 1944!

And still the war, the rotten war! The day dawns gloomy, gray, and cold; you wonder whether this furious cannon fire has an influence on the weather. Still, the hissing of the shells and nearby explosions. After lunch I convince Bernice to come on an outing around Bernières; at the same time we can get some bread at La Délivrande. There is still the bewildering river of vehicles of all sorts, channeled and directed by the specialists in red caps and white sleevecovers. They do the job — and it's no small job — with authority and skill. St-Aubin is pitiful on the ocean side; everything is collapsed, pulverized, big hole in the bell tower; in this accumulation of ruins you no longer recognize anything. Bernières is perhaps less seriously hit, except naturally, the houses on the seawall. The Geslot villa is repairable; the structure is still standing, although many shells have left visible marks all around, on the walls and trees. At sea, the huge fleet is anchored and the "ducks" come and go. The silvery balloons can be seen from close up. Moving English cemetery at Bernières, right in the sand; the crosses are already numerous, so close together and all with the same date, 6-6-44…the bloodbath of the landing!

Saw a strange piece of machinery, a huge scraper mounted on a tracked vehicle, used to flatten the terrain (*bulldozer*).

Church at Bernières badly damaged.

Tanks, trucks are hidden in all the hedges of Périers. Traveling through the district you discover them; they are unexpected surprises.

Another mass on the second floor. I attend half-asleep; it's the time of day when I usually sleep so well, when I'm able to make up for the bad hours of the night. I put my sheepskin jacket on over the sweaters that I wear at night, a beret pulled down to hide my disordered hair, barefoot in my slippers…for a "noble lady of the manor," who has her private mass in her "private chapel," I lack style!

This evening, rain. Our sergeant announces: "Much cannon tonight." It's lovely for sleeping, and terrible for those who are under it. Oh, to see the end of this obscene war, and I am so afraid that it will be a long time!

July 2, 1944

Marvelous night. I slept without waking up a single time, although it seems that at three o'clock in the morning it was banging hard. Mass at the church; many soldiers, very quiet and collected; many communions. Intense shelling and many "incoming" very close by, with that characteristic noise that you recognize immediately. At one time they were hitting so close by that the tiles were falling, and Bernice came to seek refuge at the house. Weather horribly hot and heavy.

Tonight three little tanks went for a "stroll" in the vegetable garden. The wall enclosing the park has a new and enormous breach.

Word arrives of an awful thing. Last night a bomb killed Dr. Berot and his family (?) while they were in their shelter. It's horrible! If only it could prove to be a false rumor. The mayor of Lion, Mr. Cerier, is supposed to have been killed also, in the same fashion.

July 3, 1944

Ordinary day. After dinner, for an hour, numerous shells fall behind the farm. Another milk cow killed. The hisses follow one after the other continually and seem to graze our skulls; we duck mechanically. Rain, mud. Night with sleep, despite airplane and heavy A.A.

July 4, 1944

At eleven o'clock this morning, visit to the house by two officers, one of them very young. It's going to be requisitioned in three days; for what purpose? How many rooms? They don't say. They check the thickness of the ceilings and walls.

The bulletin announces the capture of St-Jores; the road from Barneville to Carentan has been cut. Carpiquet taken. And especially, in Russia, fall of Minsk and German rout. If only the end could come quickly!

They continue with the shelter begun yesterday behind the house. It will be sizable; they're digging several deep chambers linked by corridors. It's intended for the officers.

Another visit this afternoon. Officer escorted by our sergeant. The parlor will be the mess for twelve officers and an office; they'll eat in the dining room. They're making new shelters in the vegetable garden. I learn that there are a hundred men around the house...all underground.

Seven o'clock: This evening the terrible cannon fire again takes us as its target. The "incoming" near the farm are dreadful! Will we be able to hold on?

July 5, 1944

Day marked by a memorable event...for a woman. I went to the hairdresser! I found an acceptable one at La Délivrande, and I needed so badly to feel my hair done at last! What a physical pleasure, almost a spiritual relief. It's dumb!

And yet after the session I had a shock. I went as far as Luc to catch a glimpse of the boats, and in a group that was chatting I ran across a women evacuated from Verson, which had become unbearable, and who had, according to her, left Caen on June 17. As a result she was able to give some details. I hope that her womanly emotion, having suffered horrendous fear, made her exaggerate. According to her, Caen is "entirely leveled," except for St-Etienne, the St-Martin district, and the Rue Cafonière-Bon Sauveur[15] district—six thousand dead—many people evacuated—six thousand people hiding in the tunnels of St-Etienne and others in the Vaucelles quarries. But supposedly there is not a single house standing in the heart of the city. I dare not believe such an awful thing. Where are my unfortunate friends? I am sick to think of such a horror. And my little apartment? And my things? But that's nothing compared to the rest.

Also met on the seawall a charming girl whom I sensed to be of a certain social circle. We introduced ourselves after some chatting. It was Miss Canneux, daughter of a lawyer who is the mayor of Luc (?). She told me that she had seen Marcel Dumont, subprefect of Corrèze, fleeing Caen. Dr. and Mrs. Dumont are alive, rescued from their trench after having their house fall on them. I shall try to see her again. She informed me that Logue and his daughter have been killed.

At two o'clock, arrival of my new guests: loaded trucks, unpacking of an enormous amount of equipment, setting up the kitchen, the dining room for *messieurs* the officers, and their lounge in the parlor. Deafening noise, commotion, singing, laughing, shouting, various jokes, almost like southerners. I am dumbfounded. I didn't think the English were so demonstrative. But what an army! A gong is sounded for tea and for lunch, and at five o'clock, with all work over for practical purposes, the officers are settled into easy chairs and auto cushions, reading!!

I have the feeling that I'm housing a large restaurant for "*gentlemen.*" Coming and going between the dining room and the parlor, newspapers abandoned at random, odors of cigarettes and cooking, a number of radios playing music. *Four* officers, *six* orderlies!

Four officers in the parlor, three men in the kitchen (two in a German wooden bed, the cook sleeping under the big kitchen table).

Barely a month ago I still had the others...and what a difference in their conceptions of war. When the English arrived, I found their equipment poorly kept and not very comfortable. Evidently, the "commandos" who made the landing had on their backs only what was strictly necessary, and I am reconsidering my impression of the beginning. Although they do not have a strictly prescribed uniform, and each one adds his own personal touch to it (something that would not be tolerated in the German army), they are comfortably equipped: Woolens of soft wool (not artificial), raincoats, suits to protect against gas, warm, soft blankets. In addition, much equipment devices of all kinds: gasoline motors, oil stoves, thermoses, Norwegian cookers, pipes, ropes, splendid tents, an imposing quantity of magnificent tires, and prodigal quantities of gasoline. With this there is no frugality, but rather a certain waste.

Another difference that strikes you constantly: a gaiety expressed in constant songs — not harmonious, perhaps, but suggesting youth and freedom from care; whistles, calls, and certainly jokes that I don't understand. Free men who seem to be enjoying themselves. I think of the grave young Germans, sad and mechanical, of their rare songs, melancholy but so musical. So many differences between these two peoples. We seem to be closer to the English.

Tonight we'll sleep under the stairs again, with these men in bed in the ground-floor rooms. As for the rest of the hundred men, they continue to dig in the park, in the paths, in the cyclamens, in the vegetable garden. The place is no longer anything but an immense molehill. The office-shelter behind the house is taking on unbelievable proportions, and naturally no camouflage; they'll get us spotted and killed, these bastards! What incoming shells we have taken today, and so close that Bernice and I, scared out of our wits, left our tea to seek refuge under the stairs. Even there we felt the wind from the shells, and what brutal impacts. "This not good," said our sergeant, who came to join us, I think because he feels a little sorry for us. What sort of night will we have? That doesn't stop the men from singing.

Slept badly—too much cannon fire and thinking too much about what I've heard regarding Caen.

July 6, 1944

Anniversary of the landing; it was gray and cold that day, that awful day when I watched the hardworking, disciplined, sad men who had filled the house leaving, surprised and haggard. Today is a day of relentless, blazing sunshine. The carefree men in khaki sing, whistle, loaf, wash up in the open air, putter, chop wood, or fix up their little personal areas. The officers eat (a substantial menu — soup, meat pudding, garden vegetables, cheese, jam and special crackers, coffee with milk) and say as they leave you, "*Excuse me*, I'm going to work *a little*." A little indeed, I imagine! But Verson, which had been English, is German once again, as well as the Carpiquet airfield, where, according to the latest news, the Germans are burying their tanks to camouflage them. I fear that the lofty plan announced at the arrival, "war over by Christmas," is another delusion.

I hope that I won't have to continue writing the story of this house for too many more long months. It's true that I could end up in small pieces before long. The heavy direct hits continue to fall around us: pasture with the apple trees next to the woods, large pasture at the farm, more than a hundred shells per day. We are the worst placed in the district. We shall see! I would like, though, to see how it ends (and yet the fears that I chew over at night on that subject are not funny); I would also like so much to see friends and familiar faces again.

One month now that we sleep without getting undressed and go to bed on the hard floor; pallet and mattress on the paving. But we are getting used to it, our ribs no longer hurt, and in the morning, the only time when I sleep really soundly, I roll over with pleasure on this rough bunk, in this stone shelter under the stairs.

July 7, 1944

Bad beginning to the night. Salvo after salvo from the cannons in the sector (the sergeant told me yesterday evening that there are four hundred of them) — the outgoing shells bang so loudly across from the house that you can't get a wink of sleep, except toward morning, when I sleep so soundly that I don't hear a German airplane, which supposedly made dives above us for a long time, greeted by intense A.A. Heard nothing; you get used to it.

Brainstorm of the day: *Messieurs* the officers have commanded one of their soldiers to remove the "intact" panes remaining in the ground-floor windows. Reason: "In case of bombardment, they could be wounded by the panes exploding"—!! (They are right at the front and they are at war!!) I appear as if by chance at the moment when the soldier starts to pry out the putty with a knife. I tap him on the shoulder, I say *"No good; no correct"*; he runs like a hare. A young officer who got up with difficulty at nine o'clock and who, in his pajamas, is in the process of shaving, comes out of the parlor and explains to me that it is in order to "save them"…but fortunately I know the real reason. I demand the *"interpreter-sergeant."* I find him coming out of a hole, and I explain that this winter I will not have any putty to put the panes back, that this is not *"correct,"* and that I want to speak to the *"general."*

(Later: The word has its effect; my cold demeanor must prove that I'm resolved not to let myself be trifled with. They will therefore leave the intact panes, contenting themselves with removing the broken ones, which are, alas, the more numerous. I take advantage of the situation to demand the return of two outhouse doors that had disappeared two days before, probably into a shelter, as the roof!)

Continuation and…let us hope…the end!! [end of first notebook]
[start of second notebook]

The house is vandalized a little more each day. You can no longer go up to the vegetable garden using the little path by the wall. There's nothing there anymore but caves dug under the cyclamens, which I can see thrown in all directions…when you reflect that for at least eighty years people have worked hard to protect and multiply them and that they had become an immense white and mauve carpet, covering everything from August to October! The trucks and the little tanks drive over them…

At ten-thirty this morning I was summoned by the commanding officer, who has undoubtedly been made aware of my protest about the windowpanes. The sergeant still serves as interpreter. I stood by my protest, and when he had me told that it would be dangerous if more of them should explode I wanted to laugh in his face...this well-fed "warrior" is afraid of shards of glass! I replied that it is probably the house that will explode, and that this would be much more dangerous. Since I know that he is very easily frightened, I hope that this is not going to delight him. I also stand by my protest concerning the two outhouse doors, and the good sergeant delivers a little speech; I understand from certain words that I am "demanding a *proper requisition form*." That's a scream! I would never have thought to ask for such a thing! We part company politely, but without the smile like at the beginning, after his having me told that they would comply and that the matter would be taken care of.

Aside from that, my comfort is increasing; the cook, who is an angel, gives me as much hot water as I want for my washing up, and his helpers, who have their orders, are eager to wait on me! To say nothing of everything that Bernice gleans in the way of tea, crackers, canned goods. Yesterday evening we had a marvelous cold meal, with potted liver and beef kidneys, embellished with vegetables *à la mayonnaise*...splendid. While so many poor people are probably starving on the other side of the lines, on the German side! What a situation!!

The cook went to get some cows that were killed at Beuville. He told me that six were killed and seven wounded tonight. He saw two little calves who were nuzzling their dead mother...misery!!

Bulletin not very exciting: situation unchanged around Caen.

Since yesterday, in addition to the numerous sentries in the vegetable garden, the park, and the drive, there is one at the gate (who by the way has no military bearing, most often sitting on the boundary stone). I asked the sergeant the reason. He replied ironically, "A whim," and shrugged his shoulders. He certainly has no admiration for his superiors; his twenty-two years of experience and travels throughout the world cause him to look with a natural distrust upon the two years of preparation of his young commander. For my part, I prefer a hundredfold the good sense and the imperturbability of this plump, good-hearted man to the self-satisfaction and flagrant uselessness of his commanding officer. Beauty of the military profession: the second fiddle is often splendid and the ranking officer worthless.

I saw a shell explode at the top of the drive; big spray—toll: nine killed; seven very seriously wounded! Total wounded for the day: thirty-five to forty. A shell exploded even closer; some branches torn off the walnut. One could die at any moment—

Still "incoming"; the big shells. Last night a family of four killed at Plumetot!

5:30 P.M.: I really thought that we were the chosen target! The shells were falling so close that the blast opened doors and windows. Officers left their tea abruptly, looking rather worried. I went down to the ground floor looking unconcerned…but it was an act!

I was to learn later that this evening consummated the annihilation of Caen. The bombardment on the first day of the landing, on Tuesday, June 6, had already caused enormous damage; entire streets had been destroyed, La Miséricorde[16] destroyed and burned with so many nurses (poor dear Annette), so many nuns and patients! Every day after that, bombs fell, but nothing approached the disaster of July 7. The entire city was annihilated in an apocalyptic chaos. Thousands killed, people horribly wounded, the remaining survivors destitute. There are similar examples in the course of history, but few as tragic.

Never, never will I forget that offensive of July 7! For several hours we felt it coming; six hundred men arrived in the morning. At the farm, the Red Cross arranged everything in the barns and made room.

At the house the non-commissioned officers bustled around near the offices with papers in their hands. And among the men the murmur began to spread: "Offensive for tonight." Perhaps the Germans foresaw it, because the shells fell thickly. The first trucks left crammed with men with their gear, who we knew were going up to the line. But we never could have imagined such a sight.

We were finishing dinner at eight o'clock. The batteries began barrage fire, an intense pounding; then, above their familiar clamor, we suddenly heard the long, meowing slide that had already passed over our heads on the day of the landing. It was the battleships (which had arrived, apparently, during the day) joining in. Endlessly, endlessly, their long, unmistakable hiss slid over us, just above our heads, it seemed.

And suddenly a heavy, powerful roaring reached us. All the men massed around us at the gate; all those grouped in the drive turned and greeted it with a clamor. The squadrons of bombers came in at an angle, close together, steady, massive, one following another continuously, endlessly, without a gap. It was crushing in its strength and terrifying in what one imagined of the potential death hidden in their flanks. They passed over continuously; perhaps a thousand of them passed, greeted by furious A.A. They slid with their heavy and confident flight among the fireballs of the shells; red streaks rose toward them and exploded in luminous sprays, in black plumes, but they passed without pause and the ground beneath our feet shook with the terrible weight of their bombs; the houses trembled, the doors opened, the noise of windowpanes rattling could be heard in spite of the terrifying roar. Firing by the batteries, hisses of the naval shells, crushing fall of tons of bombs, and coming toward us among the trees, then at ground level, enveloping us in an opaque, acrid vapor, the artificial clouds released to protect the tanks and infantry drowned everything in a sinister shroud. Chests tight, nerves tense, we were lost, drowned in this fog and this noise. Horrible vision of war! We were part of this sinister thing; it was in us and we were part of it, a hell of fire and noise in which we would perhaps disappear with so many others, so many innocent children, women, and men distraught with horror, so many animals mad with terror. And in this suffocation the voices of the men in khaki, men ready for the sacrifice, were a blessing to us. Edgy, excited by "great battle," proud also of these powerful English arms, their youth rose above the storm and made us pull away a little from its grip. Yet some were sad to have lost comrades killed during the day; one of them, melancholy, thinking of the English women, told me, "Mama cry"; but all were vibrant with that terrible excitement of combat. The cook spoke to me of the German bombardments of England: "Comrade lost eight people in his family, he all alone now. Comrade over there lost four children, no more children now." And this avenged the other! As for our sergeant, he exulted, "*Boches* much afraid now."

We left to lie down, still in our stair hole, of course, where fortunately the noise was slightly reduced; in my room, with the batteries opposite and not a pane in the windows, it would have been unbearable! We chatted for a long time, without sleeping. It was just an uninterrupted rumbling of cannons and the endless hisses of the naval long-range shells. What a night!! Disturbed sleep, interrupted a hundred times. Officers restless, talking, opening and closing the doors of the parlor and the hall. Hellish roaring. We talk, we doze, and so on continually, when suddenly...rran...a shell! To me it seemed so close that it must have hit the house! Windowpanes flew in shards, everything banged everywhere! It was seven o'clock in the morning and a sergeant had gone out of the house two seconds before; he had time to go to the kitchen and was hit by a big branch. We listened anxiously. Noise of someone walking on broken glass, someone talking in the kitchen, and a strong odor of gunpowder invades the house;

you sensed that all the windows and doors are open. Then every-thing quieted down. Suddenly I heard the stamping of persistent lit-tle feet behind the folding screen. I got up. It was the dog Frick, completely panic-stricken, who threw himself on our mattresses, and I didn't have the heart to send him away. He was panting, and he rolled delightedly against us, so happy to feel safe. We petted him, reassured him, talked for a while...and all three of us went back to sleep, with him puffing against my back. A cheerful voice pulled us back from sleep: "Hello, how is it going, madame?" with the expected accent. "Oh! no good sleep tonight!" It was Louis, the delightful cook, such a good sort, who was bringing us boiling-hot tea in the big enameled mugs used by the soldiers. This solicitude was delight-ful, it did us so much good, coming out of that terrible night. I thanked him and then asked him, "Where is the shell, Louis?" He answered right away, with that cheery air of his own, "House not broken, madame. Shell fallen little trees there in front." In fact it had fallen in the hedges bordering the little path, ten meters from the house.

I put off until later my inspection of the damage; one becomes so philosophical and fatalistic. I sipped my tea and ate some English crackers and slipped back under the covers for an hour.

July 8, 1944

I spent the morning gathering up the crushed glass...once again. There's not a pane left in the stairwell; in my room a hole in the ceil-ing, more broken panes, as in all the rooms on the second floor. You find dirt and walnut branches carried all the way up there! Outside, a big hole under the chestnut, which is damaged at the base this time, poor, beautiful tree, already so mutilated a month ago! Fragments have made holes in the walls of the gatehouse. The facade of my house is also pockmarked—you find big fragments everywhere; a parked truck has its rear end shredded, as well as a rear wheel; to say noth-

ing of the big drums of oil that have landed in front of the stoop, burst
open and losing their contents. It could all be so much worse—you
so fully expect to see the house down on the ground one day and
yourself under it—that you feel a relief, and a gratitude. Dear house,
little fortress that is my shelter, and perhaps my security, I love you.

From the noon report: Few details yet on the offensive, it's too
soon, and certainly it will continue for several days. They announce,
nevertheless, that 2,300 tons of shells have been fired during the
night—five villages taken back: Hérouville, Lébisey, Epron, Authie,
and one other—they're 2 km from Caen. In Manche: St-Jean-de-
Daye.

I spent the afternoon at the farm. Since this morning the ambu-
lances have been on alert and have had to ask for additional vehicles. It's just an incessant coming and going between the lines of
combat and us. The vehicles leave rapidly and return more slowly,
carefully, loaded with wounded men. What a procession; what sights!
Some lightly wounded, smoking the inevitable consolation cigarette;
others, whom they unload with the greatest possible gentleness, and
who are white as sheets, their nostrils tight, their eyes rolled back.
Wide, bleeding lacerations, shattered limbs, internal injuries, faces
in shreds…an entire poor youth martyred. Some are simply shell-
shocked and it's moving to see them sob, hiccup, supported by comrades, who walk them around in a tender, maternal way, talk to them,
try to reassure them. Their hands are shaking with convulsive tremors;
a cannon shot (one of theirs) that's too loud makes them jump and
crouch down like hunted animals. What visions of horror have their
haggard eyes recorded?

The captured Germans are placed apart, in a stable, but are exam-
ined in their turn, carried with the same careful precautions. Many
are very seriously wounded. All are dirty, their hair long, faces
unshaven, they who were so well groomed not long ago. Their long

hands, their thinness speak of the privations of this month-long siege in the Lébisey *Blockhauses* under the incessant shelling. Perhaps their status as prisoners seems sweet to them after this nightmarish night. Some throw themselves in rapture on the tea, the jam, and the crackers offered them. Twelve hours ago these men were enemies; now we support them with kind gestures.

The batteries next to us have not ceased their barrage firing for an instant all day; we're so used to it that we no longer pay any attention to it; we no longer hear it—at times!

July 9, 1944

The offensive, which lasted thirty-six hours (we were stupefied by the noise), stopped this evening. The calm and silence seemed surprising. And still it was a bad night. The German cannons started again: A shell fell in the road in front of the old farm (one Englishman on sentry duty killed). Under the stairs we were a little breathless. And then an airplane came to prowl endlessly just above our heads; it's unbearable!

Three bombs farther off. Mass at the church. Weather fair but cool.

Caen has been taken by the troops as of this morning, except for La Maladrerie (they say—?). It's a great piece of news, which must have cost dearly to the city, the civilians, and the two armies in the field. Inevitable consequence: departure of the soldiers at my house. The 42nd and the 47th leave first, for Lébisey. I meet the sergeant (our dear sergeant) in the garden at six o'clock, wearing all his gear; he tells me, and it breaks my heart! We will miss this good, imperturbable man very much. His presence has helped us to bear the horrendous times. Nothing surprised him, everything was *"nécessaire!"* I loved his humor, and the meals we shared with him were happy.

This is the law of war: to always, always see new troops march by, who, after having stayed awhile, often having created affections around themselves, leave toward their destiny. I would be very sorry if any harm came to this good man, and I ask him to correspond with us. He too is moved by his departure, and yet he is a professional who has rambled for more than twenty years.

Bad night: The cannons and the tanks surrounding us leave with a tremendous clanking. And suddenly there is an immense detonation, which seems to carry away everything in its path, shakes the house so hard with its blast that you wonder how it resists: It's the heavy pieces brought from the coast, which have been set up near us. We were used to the furious pop-guns and the antitank guns. This new noise, that ravages like a squall and makes you feel empty, is going to be pretty hard to bear.

July 10, 1944

Great bustle of departure, just like the Germans before. The trucks shuttle back and forth continually. They demolish what they took so much trouble to set up: trenches are being wrecked that took them days and days to make! This soldier's life is idiotic...so much time wasted, so many fruitless efforts. They take away everything, that which belongs to them and also that which belongs to the house; it's the eternal story! And I am weary of watching!

The unit camping in the pasture at the old farm is waiting for the departure, to move in in, its turn.

This afternoon the officers of the 43rd begin to take possession of the house with a noisy cheerfulness and jokes that approach mindlessness. They asked me for a piano...again! I hope that this is not a bad sign! The Germans were looking for one on the very eve of the landing...I hope that this piano idea on the part of this group doesn't bring us bad luck! A piano! While a few miles away the battle rages, Caen is not completely freed, and twice this morning German airplanes flew over and machine-gunned us. They're crazy!!

Tiring afternoon, a hundred requests per hour. They knock at my door, they busy themselves with the gasoline motor, they ask for a broom, hot water for shaving, etc.... all of it, I should say, with unfailing good humor. You want to think of the sadnesses of this war, and at times you laugh, caught up as you are by this exuberance. You are carried along on a tide of life! Some Scotsmen have set up camp behind the vegetable garden; I pay them several visits; they are charming. Everything swarms, everything moves continuously: stream of trucks, motorcycles, men moving around creating shelters, dragging their equipment, whistling and singing. Everything is just a vast camp where Life is mistress, sovereign, heedless of Death and the roaring guns!

July 11, 1944

I go to Luc in the afternoon; of course, I have only one thought: to find evacuees from Caen and get some information. At the Hotel Estival I run across Mr. Lachaise, who tells me that his wife arrived the previous evening after thirty days spent in Caen in a cellar. As I am rejoicing at the idea of questioning him, two cyclists pass by, and I recognize Dr. Lachappelle. I jump on my bicycle and run after them. Recognition, explanations; I finally begin to get details, which are, I must say, quite distressing! We leave together to take a tour as far as La Brèche; this is the first time that he has come, and he wants to see the spectacle of the boats. We chat endlessly of everything and everyone; I learn for certain of the annihilation of almost all of Caen, of the death of so many people, including, to my horror, one of the Montard women!! He thinks it is the elder. I am shattered. On returning to Cresserons we part, to take different routes, but I decide to go the next day to Caen. I hope to get through, and I am in too much of a hurry to see some of the survivors and look for friends.

Night marvelously quiet. I sleep.

July 12, 1944

Leave Périers at ten o'clock, pass through Beuville, heavily damaged, Biéville even more so, Lébisey shattered, with the trees of the woods like burned posts. On the sides of the road the traces of the battle: broken rifles, abandoned equipment, German and English mess tins lying together, punctured by bullets. Graves on the edge of the road (one so shallow that boots and shoes stick out), a little cross hastily made, a helmet. On the plateau, the isolated farm on the right is a ruin and a strong odor of rot comes from it: dead animals. I understand that it's useless to approach Caen by way of Le Gaillon or Le Vaugueux, and I take the Chemin aux Boeufs, following the imprint of the tracked vehicles on the ground. On the shoulder, a German corpse lies in its green tunic, the red ribbon of Russia gleaming, surrounded by flies. At the bottom of the hill, first sight of the collapsed houses; I question some unfortunates digging in the rubble of what was their property. They tell me not to go to Caen, that it's being fired on today, that in any case all the streets are impassable, that one must skirt around. I start off again to the left, by the Rue d'Hérouville; still following the tracks of the tanks, I cross former pastures pitted with craters, orchards without enclosing walls, vegetable gardens that must have been very beautiful, where Tommies are camped. I pass by a chapel that I don't recognize (I found out later that I had crossed the Carmelite property).

I find the road from Ouistreham covered with a thick layer of dust; I take it to the right to reach the Place Reine-Mathilde. St-Gilles's is nothing but a heap of gravel, from which two interior arches emerge — La Trinité is standing; the Rue des Chauvines is impassable. I go down Rue le Manissier, Rue Basse is impassable; it's chaos. I continue by way of back streets. (In one of them I run across the first human that I've met in this desert. It's "Claude," the salesman from the Salle des Ventes. We recognize each other; he says to me,

"They are our saviors, they have delivered us." Yes, of course…but at what a price!)

Place Courtonne, some facades standing, but nothing behind; the quays are blocked off, a shapeless heap. I take the Boulevard des Alliés; the central market is standing, but collapsed on the inside; the opposite side where the stores were is nothing but a long suc-cession of charred ruins. Place St-Pierre is an unforgettable sight: I am alone, the silence is complete, and I contemplate the desolation. The slender, airy spire of St-Pierre's no longer exists. The Escoville House, that marvel, is destroyed; the houses surrounding the square no longer exist; the entrance to Rue St-Jean is a chaotic heap of blocks, from which emerges, detached from the rest, the silhouette of St-Jean's. No point in trying to venture that way; it would be a mountain-climbing session that would take hours. Same horrible spectacle around the Rue de Geöle, where I decide to give up the idea of finding my friends; one cannot live in this jumble of collapsed walls. I am still alone in this square, formerly so lively, and I am gripped by anguish. I leave, following the Boulevard, where every-thing is burned and broken up all the way to the Place du Théâtre. The Marlettes' building is an open shell where everything has burned, as is the theater. Only a black cat prowling. The Rue des Jacobins is a chaos.

I come to the Préfecture, where I find a few people alive. Rue St-Pierre, the Auchin building is intact; I approach. I ask for infor-mation from a D.P.,[17] and suddenly a cyclist comes up; it's Robert. He's the first of the crowd that I've found. He contemplates the facade of his building, where a shell has made a round hole this morning. Then he leads me to his sister's place, in the only neigh-borhood that is still almost intact. There I find the Marlettes and Catherine. Long explanations, inquiries, and details about every-body; heartbreaking news.

We go together to Bon Sauveur to see Marlene, who has lost an eye and whose father has been killed. She is in a wretched condition, physically and mentally. The Montards are staying in the Rue Caponnière. I fall into the arms of Mr. Lignoir, who climbs through a window, the door being unusable. He is thin and changed, but energetic, and springs from the house. Mimi...since yesterday I had thought she was dead, and in a flash I realize that it is Annette who has been killed, the dear, adorable girl, so industrious, so courageous, so alive. My heart is heavy with grief! I loved her so much; her charm, her personality had always captivated me. How sad! I hold back the words that might betray my thoughts, but Mimi has understood with one glance that I know everything, and her emotion, like mine, is intense. Hollow eyes, a face that shows suffering.

Unexpected and comforting lunch at the Dorts' with the Marlettes. I leave to look for other survivors. Mrs. Jouan in bed at Bon Sauveur, physically and spiritually destitute. Everything lost: house, comforts, life of security and almost luxury, in the house where she had always lived. Lived to the age of eighty-two, to suffer this! Saw Pierre, Mustier, her husband, and her kid homeless; Breton; Perrin. Saw Madeleine Lignoir-Montard, wounded by a recent shell and in bed in a ward, thinner in her rough hospital gown. We understand each other without needing to speak, and she knows that I am grieving for Annette. Saw the Maltemps—Juliette had left with an ambulance and gotten lost behind the German lines around Trun, along with Lazot.

The incoming shells are frequent: Bon Sauveur this morning; Place St-Martin. When I leave, from around the Palais de Justice, it's banging hard. The sector isn't secure this evening, and I'm a little scared, in this loneliness with the hissing. I retrace the route, at one point getting lost in the chaos of Rue Basse. Fatigue, insurmountable sadness. All night without sleeping I replay this spectacle of horror; I go over the list of the dead. It's even more horrible than I had thought, and it's so enormous that it's hard to grasp!

—LaRue-Geslot-Minard reunited at Amayé—everything lost.

—André—everything lost, after having changed shelters several times and fled the danger. Everything lost.

—Mother Marlette-Escher-Lebrun—everything lost.

—Annette Valentin—everything lost.

—Mrs. Dubois, Yvette—everything lost.

—All the doctors in the center of Caen (except Bonnet)—everything lost.

—Mrs. Duval killed.

—Mr. and Mrs. Michel still under the rubble with the Delbourges.

—La Miséricorde—seventeen nuns killed, numerous people not yet recovered, including Annette...

—Gerard-Fenice household two children killed at Evrecy.

—Le Rasle—one child killed, one child blinded, all wounded.

—Degasse murdered on a road (?) 50,000 francs on him, stolen.

—A doctor nearby: thirteen children, all killed.

—Hallette household—young woman, little girl killed.

The English are talking about having a party tomorrow evening!... I could kill them...

Unforgettable day. Dantean spectacle of war: foul, cruel and unjust. Never will I forget...

July 13, 1944
Numerous incoming shells. Irritating bagpipes all day long.
Soirée organized by *messieurs* the officers. Big party! Reason: arrival of the canteen, whiskey and beer...of course, a party is called for!! Three girls from La Délivrande, nurses, were invited. So was I, the day before. They borrowed twenty-four glasses from me. The commanding officer, escorted by the Scotsman who speaks French, came

in person to get me. Extreme courtesy, obligatory whiskey, plate of ham and vegetables, numerous cigarettes. Those who speak French are eager to do so; conversations (some of them interesting, especially one with the colonel, who, through the interpreter, asks me numerous questions about de Gaulle, politics, the government that France hopes for, maintaining order, etc.). I do my best to give them the impression of a Frenchwoman who is both lighthearted and serious-minded, and I weigh my words. I sense that I am being closely observed. The commanding officer has me thanked (for what?); the colonel has me told that I should express my wants if I am unhappy with anything...

All very English, with a boundless courtesy. Some officers very pleasant; a charming Welshman; everyone in very good spirits. The nurses, distant at first, become human and talk with me very pleasantly. At eleven o'clock I take my leave of the commanding officer, offer my thanks, and take off. The singing has begun, under the influence of the numerous whiskeys, and since it's very ugly and I've had enough of it, I leave. (I think of the beautiful German songs, of the voices in tune and full of nuances, the acute musical sense, the emotion!) At that moment, the Scottish bagpiper arrives. From the gate I watch a wild ballet (village dance style) in front of the stoop, led by the bagpipe. We shall have seen everything in this house!

Bernice decides not to go to bed under the stairs while there is so much singing and noise. Until two o'clock they bray, talk, rush around! A staggering return to the second floor causes the big clock in the linen room to fall! Lovely! That and five broken glasses, one mirror frame, hardware torn off the chest of drawers!!!

July 14, 1944!!! [Bastille Day]

Uneventful, but with reflections that are more than melancholy. Numerous airplanes passed over, intense machine-gunning, airplanes shot down. Numerous incoming shells. Looks like it will be a lovely night.

July 15, 1944

Pleasant surprise to see the Colbert family arrive this morning, temporarily staying at Hélène Montblanc's, and hoping to move to Caen. After a fruitless search in the district, where everything is occupied, I decide to give them the third floor of the house, which, after being cleaned and fixed up, could house them and leave them their independence. Second surprise: Laura M. comes to tell me that they have arrived at Mathieu and that her mother is expecting me to change the dressings of her wounds. I run over there in the afternoon. They are cooped up on the second floor at the farm. I talk with Madeleine for a long time...how sad, everything she tells me... and everything she doesn't!!

Mr. Lignoir is magnificently energetic. I leave with my heart heavy to see them dispossessed of everything, without one piece of furniture, in that home that used to be so full of beautiful things, books, scientific collections.... Nothing here any longer, nothing but ruins in the Rue de Geôle, Annette killed; it's really too much!! Poor Madeleine.

July 16, 1944

Yesterday I asked for permission to go to the *Blockhauses* to look for my folding bedstead, which was taken by the Germans. Two soldiers go with me. I'm received by a Scottish officer in a short skirt: tall, thin, distant, and polite. I can't find my bed, and am told that it was destroyed by the shelling...the first answer was that it was being used by an officer, and I continue to believe that's the truth; but I don't insist, and I ask whether I can have one that is there in a tent and is in fairly bad shape anyway. The officer gives orders, and

I leave in a car with two soldiers and the shabby bed that doesn't belong to me. I learn of the deaths of Elisabeth and Némy, killed with twenty-eight people in the shelter across from the Vaugueux clinic. Her sister is supposed to have been evacuated with her two little children to Cresserons. I shall go tomorrow.

Four times today I had to advise these soldiers that the telephone was ringing…nobody is in charge of the phone; everybody eats or sleeps without worrying about it.

The action since yesterday evening is violent at Vaucelles, which is being shelled by both belligerents. Numerous shells hit Caen.

Today quiet, without incidents. The situation around Caen remains unchanged; it's been so long!

July 17, 1944

Saw Mrs. Juliard, Elisabeth's sister, at Cresserons. Numerous details about Caen and all the dead. Awful! Saw Madeleine at Mathieu. On my return I find walls collapsed in Périers; since this morning shells have been falling ceaselessly between the road to Beuville and us. Three in the drive. Lovely! Unpleasant feeling of insecurity. Tanks everywhere.

July 18, 1944

Another offensive, and on what a scale! Began in the night with the noise of 105s; their blast seems to carry everything away. Then continually, for hours, tanks passed with a tremendous clanking; it seemed as if it would never stop. And at five-thirty there began this hellish cannon fire that roared, tremendous, until ten o'clock, thick and fast, a merciless pounding by pieces of all calibers, whose different voices you could distinguish. I found out later that *two thousand* tanks participated in this gigantic battle. And then, as always, this was followed by the arrival of the squadrons that make the earth tremble under the weight of their bombs. Someone said *six thousand* airplanes! The bombardment lasted fifty-five minutes. Six thousand tons of explosives dropped. Anything is possible, it was so hellish. The brunt of the effort was directed against Colombelle, which has held out since the beginning and which was plastering us these days with its artillery pieces. An immense battle, gigantic and ferocious; one more horror, new sorrows, horrible sufferings to add to the list!

The officers have left the house for the firing line. Only the supply officer, the sergeant-major, and some soldiers remain. Since my complaint about a theft from the linen room armoire, we're not on speaking terms.

This evening the bulletin still doesn't say anything.

There were "incoming" all day. The cannon fire continues, but not as close together as this morning.

July 19, 1944

Morning trip to Mathieu in company with the Colberts. In the fields, the incoming shells fall 200 meters behind us.

Afternoon: trip to the sea. Contemplated the huge crater where the Berot family and seventeen persons were killed by the magnetic mine. Another mine fell near the Bosts'. Everything is ravaged and blown down over a wide area. Met Larusse, saw R. Juliard.

As I was leaving, I was obliged to stop on the ridge at Périers to let twenty tanks pass, leaving for the attack toward the Orne. Twenty meters away, one following the other in a steady stream, turrets open; they passed, massive and powerful, in an immense tornado of yellow dust rising toward the clouds. It was impressive. At a distance, one can locate all the roads from the swirls of this tremendous dust raised by every truck. And since there is constant traffic on all the roads, each truck and each tracked vehicle a few meters from the next ones, a thick haze of suspended dust covers the entire countryside. A picture of war, with the incessant sound of cannons and tank battles, an unbroken rumble that absorbs everything.

July 20, 1944

Bad night, with airplanes, bombs, flashes, and wrenching outgoing fire from the heavy pieces. You feel hollowed out by all this tremendous noise and these airplanes, evil beasts searching for their prey, gripping your heart with despair.

Morning at Mathieu—afternoon without incident, except for airplanes going over, dropping explosives that whistle loud and low and bang sharply. Barely time to get to shelter. Violent thunderstorm, which may knock down the thick dust that covers everything and burns the unfortunate trees, already so ill-treated by the shells. Tank battle in the direction of Caen and east on the Orne.

Advance announced in the bulletin: Bourguébus, Cagny.

Also announced, dynamite attack against *Hitler*, who is burned and shaken up—officers with him wounded, one killed.

The attempt against Hitler is later confirmed, and it is an indication of disintegration. Speech by the Führer—police measures. May this first crack be followed by a collapse that would stop this war, which is going to destroy everything in France. Yesterday's storm continues as a drenching rain. The roof being a collection of holes, it rains as much on the third floor as in the garden—you'd need an umbrella. As for the outbuildings, since there is no longer any roof at all, they are drowned. Day without incident. Little cannon fire. The shells continue to plaster Caen.

July 22, 1944

Situation unchanged—still waiting. Certain officers who had left the house to go on the offensive have returned to rest. I think that rests are frequent in the English army. I run into the colonel, the doctor, and two or three others. They are sleeping at the house.

Outing to La Délivrande, where I run into the midwife Mrs. Leton, and Mrs. Louise DePuys, whose mother has been killed and who has just spent a month in the Fleury quarries. Met Miss Canneux, who has at her place many people evacuated from Caen, whom I shall go to see before long. More incoming shells at Périers, forty-eight days after the landing.

Bulletin not very appealing.

July 23, 1944

Loss of St-Martin-Esquay. Quiet day; almost no more noise of cannon fire. They seem to be waiting for something?

July 24, 1944

It was probably a new offensive that we sensed yesterday. Today it announced itself by a massive movement of transports of every sort: a stream of trucks, small track vehicles, motorcycles, etc.; and by the departure of the 43rd, which has been staying at the house since the fourteenth — and also, naturally, by incoming shells and by a very rough night, with airplanes, bombs, and the heavy piece whose blast ravages everything in the house. Impossible to get a wink of sleep, the airplanes flying over, A.A., and bombs are unending. It's a dreadful night.

At Luc, saw Mrs. Martin, the two Berot girls, Dr. Fenice, his son, Mrs. Leton, and on the road met Guillaume, his wife, and the Corots. With Fenice, conversation on politics and worries regarding domestic movements. He is certainly one of his family…you would think you were listening to his father, but without the same breadth. Progressive ideas. Criticizing everything, embittered. Has lost everything: his wife, his house, his livelihood (for now). In his garden, the bomb killed: his wife, his mother, the two Gerards, husband and wife, and two of their children; only the last little girl is left: three years old.

I decide to go to Caen tomorrow, despite the rumors going around about the shells raining on it.

July 25, 1944

After very bad night: departure and trip to Caen without incident. You see the flashes of the cannons, on the slopes on either side of the Orne, thundering on the eastern front. This time I go down the Côte du Calvaire. Ruins everywhere. Le Vaugueux is pitiful, and I stop for a moment in front of poor Elisabeth's house. Farther down, a few houses very sick but still standing; a few rare civilians. Rue St-Jean is free. I look for Rue de l'Engamerie without finding it, as well as Rue Jean-Romain. I don't recognize anything. Instead of going straight, Rue St-Jean turns abruptly to the left in front of a mountain of gravel. I had a very hard time recognizing Rue Singer. I go back up Rue St-Jean, take the demolished Rue St-Pierre all the way to the Blanc house.

I forgo for the time being, as too discouraging, the search for my house and what was my little apartment.

Two huge piles of rubble indicate the Dumont and Bonaire houses. Rue Singer goes as far as the square, where a policeman tells me that I can't go any farther.

Toward the Auchin house I meet Mrs. Charles. We're talking when suddenly there is a terrific crash above our heads: A shell falls on the roof of the house across from us, a few meters away. We dash into a corridor. It's not a pleasant feeling. I head toward Place St-Martin. At the moment when I come up to Marlette on the sidewalk: rran...another shell a hundred meters away. It's more and more unpleasant, even more so because these are large calibers. Conversation with Lucille, Catherine. I leave by the Avenue de Courseulles, which for two weeks has suffered badly. Saw the Maltemps, Edith Broyard, the high school, Mrs. Brielle, Isabelle, who is desolate. I come back to have lunch with the Marlettes. In the afternoon, visit to the Gerards, then I leave with Catherine and Jacques to look for the remains of what was my apartment. A climb up onto the gravel that borders the street, then we contemplate the disaster! Of a stout four-story house, there remains one and a half meters of rubble!! A search in Ernesto's former digs, amusing finds: powder and rouge still usable, although scorched. All that is quite melancholy! Corpses remain under many houses, and the stale and nauseating odor fills the air; leaving via the Place de la Mare, I learned that they had just disinterred a woman and her two children and the air was filled with a foul odor. Le Gaillon is pitiful to see, as is the street that continued behind the water-mill by the quarries. Huge shell holes, charred skeletons of trees; it's a lunar landscape that fills the heart with a bleak desolation. Stopped twice on the road for verification of my identity card; soldiers smiling and conciliatory, no problem.

July 26, 1944

Departure for Bayeux, accompanied by Louis Moreau. The route is terribly difficult because of the transports that meet you and pass you continually. The shoulders of the road are like a roller coaster, and it's both tiring and dangerous. On the sides, in all the fields, an immense, fantastic amount of equipment is accumulated. There is everything, in gigantic proportions; it's stupefying! Many burned and damaged tanks in repair areas. At Bayeux it's a mob of trucks, tanks, tracked vehicles, soldiers of every branch, nurses in khaki, in gray, in blue, evacuated civilians. There's an infernal clatter and an unbelievable mob in the long paved street that crosses the city. The English are hurrying to create a belt of wide freeways that will be reserved for use by the troops, in order to reduce congestion. You run into all of Caen.

Met the Andrés, Paul, Mrs. Bonaire, Mrs. Pinard, and Miss Suberon, one of the Malroux (the sister Jeanne was killed). Saw Mrs. Jouan, pitiful and still demanding, Marlene and her mother. Spotted lots of familiar faces; you can't stop everyone, you'd never be done.

Coming back by the Bayeux road, we are stopped at Bretteville-l'Orgueilleuse by the police, a motorcyclist who is pleasant, actually, and who leads us to the police station (civilian affairs) in a local house. Lost a half hour; they let us go after explanations, telling us not to go again without an authorization. Return to Périers at eight-thirty, gray with dust, rather tired, but pleased.

July 27, 1944

Quiet day. Only thing to report: going to see Madeleine Montard at Mathieu, I run into a deployment of police, cars, a parade of armed soldiers!!! The reason: General Montgomery is there, and we watch everything from a second floor window. Reception in the main court-yard in front of a small flag, presentation of the officers, and behind the house, he awards decorations to twenty-seven soldiers. Large ceremonial square formation. Two policemen on either side of the stoop, table with the decorations, a non-commissioned officer calling each man.

The general shakes each man's hand, decorates him, speaks to him for some time, shakes his hand again. Each man salutes, stiff and rather awkward and sometimes comical. The general mounts the stairs, the men are called and come in a disorderly way to group themselves around. Rather long speech. All very simple, with none of the rigid bearing or the enormous display of security and pomp that the Germans would have demanded in such a case. They left us to watch in peace—that says it all. He himself is plain, face thin and delicate, body rather skinny, black beret, few gestures, no stiff attitude, no apparent arrogance, probably nice. A soldier told me lovingly: "A wonderful general!"

Cinema set up in the barn at the old farm; three shows per day. They bring soldiers in trucks from just about everywhere.

July 28, 1944

Ordinary day. Go to Cresserons to ask for an authorization to go to Caen. Found "civilian affairs," a difficult officer and a charming woman in uniform. (Born in Japan, French, probably married to an Englishman, owns property near Fontainebleau, very nice, told me that she would visit next Friday.)

July 29, 1944

For the first time today and yesterday, inspection of the guard. They line up poorly and there is none of the Germans' unity of movement.

On the bulletin: The Americans are advancing in Manche; the English pulling back south of Caen.

I go to a show at the cinema set up in the barn. Poor visibility and idiotic film, uninteresting newsreel! If it's for this they bring that flood of troops by truck every day...

You hear the cannon fire. This evening there is a blaze in the direction of Caen!

July 30, 1944

Sunday. Weather still unpleasant, at times cold and at others stormy.

I try to go to bed in my room, but after a moment I go back down under the stairs; that's where I like it best...who would have imagined it, before! In my room without windowpanes, I can hear the noise and see the flashes too well. And I have gotten into the habit of curling up in this little stone shelter, where I sleep very well, now, on the hard floor. How about that!

At four o'clock, visit from "civilian affairs." The charming woman again, escorted by a fat officer, who is very clever and who seems to understand the situation and the mentality of the "undesirables" of the district. I am to go see them next Sunday.

July 31, 1944

Quiet day. The men are playing soccer!—taking the sun cure—it's the good life.

Inspection of the guard in the evening! Priceless! Soldiers out of an operetta, exaggeratedly rigid, awkward in their movements, lacking any unity. You want to laugh.

Noisy night. Heavy-piece firing, and numerous "incoming." Saw during the day, passing over Mathieu, a "pilotless airplane" or "buzz bomb."

August 1, 1944

Saw Elisabeth's sister at Cresserons.

Very hard night; numerous "incoming."

August 2, 1944

Trip to Caen; stopped twice on the way for verification of my papers. Saw Alvanne over by the old Vaugueux cemetery, whose graves and cypresses are ravaged. Saw Hubert, Beaufort, Homard, Pierre, Cassard, the Gerards, the Marlettes. Visit to Rue de l'Engamerie. Went up the new street created by the English, which runs from the Boulevard des Alliés to Place Singer. You no longer know where you are; you recognize nothing anymore in these ruins, in these charred sections of wall where you can still make out the lovely arch of a vaulted door, the silhouette of a dormer that was probably a recognized architectural treasure, the circle of a winding staircase. Thick walls of the old medieval, renaissance, or eighteenth-century homes. They rise abruptly from the heaps of rubble, in their crumbling and sinister beauty, and evoke all the past that has been shattered by the bombs of today's civilization!!

August 3, 1944

Accident happened to Jean Maltemps. The tractor that he was driving was blown up by an English mine, throwing him a long way and cutting the tractor in half. He is wounded in the foot, the arm, and the head. He should have been killed on the spot...the blast was terrible. The English had supposedly cleared the area of mines!

August 4, 1944

Better nights; fewer shells in the sector. The sky, from eleven o'clock at night on, is still illuminated by sinister red flashes and the cannon fire still thunders, but you feel that things are quieter nevertheless.

August 5, 1944

Big advance by the American armies toward Brest. In the field supposedly cleared of mines, where Maltemps's tractor blew up, the English dig up another five mines—that's reassuring! The English insist that we continue the harvest—"You have to do it, at the risk of your lives"...they're delightful!

August 6, 1944, Sunday

For the second time (last Sunday and today), a Protestant service in the open air, under the catalpa in full bloom, an immense white bouquet. Psalms and hymns sung in chorus, accompanied by an accordionist. After the Catholic mass being celebrated for two weeks on the second floor, here are the Protestants in the open air! Afternoon taken up by the invitation received in Cresserons from "civilian affairs." Extremely likeable group—Mrs. Deschamps, charm itself; the major, a Cassé sort, very funny; three women who speak French well (French women, for that matter, volunteers with the English); women officers. Plenty of tea, served simply in the kitchen. Gaiety, unaffected courtesy, very attentive, gift from the major. In spite of my protestations, they keep me there for the evening, movie at eight o'clock under a tent; there was even talk of dinner afterward, but they take me, as well as my bicycle, back in a Jeep. We start out by getting lost among the trails, then rediscover the route, taking the turns at top speed. Fog, black sky, everything is drowned in a sad mist, where from time to time you can make out the flashes of the guns. Horribly sad landscape; it's hard to make out the road; it feels like war. You meet no one but the sentries at the crossroads. Excellent evening. I invited them for after dinner the day after tomorrow to drink some Anjou wine.

August 7, 1944

Quiet day. In the afternoon, arrival of Catherine. Sad revelations.

Around eleven o'clock, offensive: cannon fire and very heavy air bombardment (a thousand airplanes), east of the Orne and south of Caen; everything trembles. The sky is just a succession of flashes; the noise is oppressive! More, still more human lives being sacrificed. (We find out later that as a result of an 8 km "error," bombs fell at Colombelles, where there was no one but Americans. Six hundred killed; four hundred wounded! English explanation: first airplane, hit by A.A., released its bombs to lighten itself, and the others thought that was the signal for the proper place!)

August 8, 1944

Preparations for the "soirée," which was very pleasant. Mrs. Deschamps arrived, escorted by the major and two officers. We settled into the former linen room, after a visit to the park and the garden. Lots of gaiety, thanks to everyone; and especially thanks to one of the officers who is none other than Kennedy, the well-known author. He is inimitable. Magic tricks with cards; incredible dexterity. A singer and mime, he is extraordinary. The mayor drank like a hole in the ground, and got high. They left late, very pleased, delighted, and it's understood that tomorrow one of the officers will come to get us at eleven o'clock in the morning to go by car to Bayeux! Great!

August 9, 1944

Bayeux: much coming and going between hospitals to find Mrs. Dessard. Around three o'clock we go to Marlene's, where we find Mrs. Dubois and Yvette and where, a half hour later, appears… Christophe!! All unexpected and peculiar. Trips going and returning very jolly, in the car with this charming officer who speaks a picturesque French, with amusing gestures, a mischievous attitude, an infectious gaiety. Childish jokes, singing, etc., and driving the car with a speed and abruptness that throw you in every direction. Horrible dust!

August 10, 1944

Departure of the 40th, which has been here since the twenty-fourth of July. Everything empties out: vegetable garden, park, house; the colonel on the third floor is still here. The house looks dismal, broken-down and dirty, as are the garden and the park, where flies swarm over the camp's rubbish. No more coming and going of noisy men, no more radio, no more singing, no more trucks. No doubt about it — in its current state this house is tolerable only as a barracks.

Rough night; numerous airplanes dropping flares, tracer bullets, searchlights, bombs, etc. English bomber squadron.

August 11, 1944

Implacable heat. At two o'clock our young driver arrives to invite us to dinner on behalf of Mrs. Deschamps. He will come to get us at six o'clock: "I will come with transportation." He is quite amusingly picturesque. Priceless account of a difference that he had yesterday with his colonel over his sloppy dress—"no hat"—impossible to recount!

Also impossible to recount was this soirée! Warm welcome in Kennedy-Smith's auto-trailer! This trailer has everything, from a bed with a garnet-red silk quilt, to a chest of drawers, a Louis XVI-style table, a chiffonier, a radio, and an accordion. All crammed with expensive cigarettes, chocolate, and especially whiskey and gin, and we partook liberally of it all. Introduction of numerous officers, including the colonel. Gin. Then we went to the officers' mess hut. Good dinner, impeccably served by two barmen in white jackets. I was between the major and the colonel. Catherine, naturally beside Tricket. After dinner they took out the tables and—quite unexpected—we danced, led by a remarkable pianist and by Kennedy, who played the accordion, sang, howled, mimed, filled the air with his presence. Great gaiety, childish, infectious, basically very nice, but what insouciance! No one thinks about war or fighting or death...and still! (They drink like sponges; it's insane what they can absorb. Cigarette after cigarette. Enough to make you deathly ill. They hold up well—you can see that they're used to it—but they're all terribly high, not far from the notorious "staggering.") Returned during the night (around midnight) with Tricket, who tried to explain to me that he is a "very serious" man. He was above all very bleary. The two of us as well. After he left, we talked for a long time, and I explained how I felt...but how difficult it is to understand another person sometimes...

August 12, 1944

We sleep off the soirée. In the afternoon, a little bicycling in the direction of Lion. Shells hissing. Cannon fire during the night. The colonel and his two orderlies are still here, forgotten, I think, until the end of the war. It must not be a loss for the army. He seems stupid, slow-witted; he spends his days vaguely reading, wandering, and indulging in painful attempts at conversation with me: "*très chère*" [very dear] for "*très chaud*" [very hot], "*roumain*" [Romanian] for "*rumeurs*" [rumors].

August 13, 1944

At the beginning of the afternoon, visit from Tricket and Kennedy, who come to invite us for the evening, to dine and go to the cinema. They come around six o'clock to get us in a car. Much quieter; a little under the weather. Light dinner in the trailer: one course. Idiotic cinema; saw Mrs. Deschamps. Return at eleven-thirty. More childish conversations.

Also, visit from "our" Sergeant Smith, who came from Bayeux, borrowing cars to make the trip. Great pleasure to see this nice fellow again.

August 14, 1944

Marvelous weather. The house is still empty; no new unit. Only the colonel is here, with his orderlies and his car. Still idle, still polite. It is strange, all the same, that a colonel, two men, and a huge car should remain forgotten in this house. What disorder I imagine in this army! The news is good, but no more radio, because the trucks have left.

August 15, 1944

Night very rough and noisy. German airplanes. Intense A.A. that explodes directly over the roofs, numerous bombs not very far away, cannon that seem closer. All rather impressive, a return to the first weeks.

After mass at Mathieu, visit with Catherine to the châteaus of Le Londel. It's deplorable! What a picture of war, all just 2 km from Périers. I find out the extent to which I have been prctected. The Flaichet château is split open by shells, gutted; the inside is sinister, in an indescribable disorder, its few pieces of furniture shattered; on the walls one or two large paintings remain, pictures of ancestors. You can discern its former beauty: pretty staircase with wrought-iron handrail, but the stones are broken, and there is a big hole between floors. Some beautiful woodwork, sculpted fireplaces, old small-paned windows, all blown apart.

At the end of the garden, two cemeteries, one English, one German: names and dates, helmets and crosses. On one German cross the dates of birth and death indicate a child of nineteen years...how sad!

The Bressier château no longer exists, all that's left is one section of wall. The stones that remain are nothing more than a pile, which they are in the process of hauling away, probably for roads. These châteaus are surrounded by pitifully shattered, burned trees, sinister skeletons, hideous stumps, all that's left of beautiful parks, noble avenues.

August 16, 1944

Noisy night, airplanes, A.A., a few "incoming," but overall the cannon fire is getting farther away. The men camped around the house go away, one after another; the transports on the roads decrease. It won't be long before Périers returns to its solitude, and that will perhaps be sad from several points of view; one will be stuck here with nothing but the pitiful inhabitants of the place.

August 17, 1944

Visit to Caen. Saw the Tabernière house, the bank, had lunch with the Cassards and Santerres, saw Juliette Varron, Gallin, the Palais de Justice, the LaRues' house (!!)

Return by way of Rue du Magasin aux Poudres. The Protestant cemetery is an unspeakable chaos! Craters one next to the other, and rising out of that, tombstones, pieces of markers, the remains of gates. Of the beautiful cypresses, old trees that made restful paths, nothing is left but burned skeletons. The Osmont graves are (perhaps) intact, but it's impossible to be sure, as a layer of hardened earth covers the stones, and then it's difficult to see the layout in this sinister disorder. On either side of the street you can see the quarries, whose walls, ravaged by the bombs, fall straight into the depths, where you can make out what used to be a bed, a pallet, a cradle, hanging from the rock. Gutted houses, pieces of walls! A Dantean picture, in a nightmarish solitude and silence.

I come back by way of La Folie and Epron, both devastated. I get lost in the trails made by the army, and for a long time I wander, lost, going for miles without seeing a human being. Nothing but the remains of crashed airplanes, cemeteries for tanks and cannons returned from battle in woeful condition and waiting to be salvaged. Solitude and sadness in these plots of ground that were the scenes of so much feverish activity, where the voice of the cannon roared for so long. Ammunition is still laid out beside trenches emptied of men. I come back to Périers, exhausted by so many sights, so many miles, and too many thoughts.

MARIE-LOUISE OSMONT'S GLOSSARY

A glossary of the Franco-German "language" that serves to explain and resolve all situations:

At the head of the list, naturally, is *nix*, which is probably a popular derivation of the *nicht* [*nichts*] that I learned in my childhood, and which is used for everything; it's the almost inevitable response to all German questions.
"Do you have eggs, milk?" *Nix.*
"I would like some chairs." *Nix.*
"*Promenade* today?" *Nix.*
"*Beaucoup* work?" *Nix.*
"*Nix* good," "*nix* mademoiselle," "*nix* eat," etc., etc…it means everything.

Grand malheur [great misfortune], which expresses everything from simple disappointment to the deepest suffering: a flat tire, a whole lot of mud, a torn suit, shoes with holes, a lost object, a slight wound, but also a death—*grand malheur*.

Kaput is used to describe both small and large things: a wrecked bicycle or car, a sweater, a plate is *kaput*, but also a dead comrade or relative.

Prima indicates satisfaction, bliss. A useful object, a good meal, a *promenade*, a pretty girl (sometimes an ugly one, for that matter), a letter received, the blessed *urlaube* [leave] so fondly anticipated, everything is *prima*.

Égal [egal] denotes both equality between two objects or two feelings, and indifference. In the first case one also says *même chose* [same thing]. The words are alike in French and German; one uses "*égal*" to refer to two objects of the same shape or the same use. But if you say to a soldier, "Not good, this officer?" he may answer with a shrug of the shoulders: "*Égal.*"

If you lend an object to a soldier, do not forget to say to him, "*Retour*" [return], with a pantomime indicating that you very much expect it. And he will answer you with a heartfelt "*retour.*" And very often, I must say, he will scrupulously return it.

Carrousel is a big party, a big spree, and especially a big drinking bout. Every day you hear, with an air of rapturous longing, "War over, *carrousel,*" and that means everything that they promise themselves in the way of celebration on that blessed day. (It's their own way of forgetting, of doping themselves, of bearing this war that is terrible for them as well.) But a comrade who comes lurching in with his mouth dry is *carrousel.* They readily admit, "Yesterday evening, officer, *beaucoup carrousel.*"

There is the *promenade*, which they propose with an inviting smile, and which is intended to suggest a plain, more or less romantic, walk, a way of passing the time and cutting the boredom, but which also suggests...everything and more!

Naturally, there is the *oh là là!* that every woman in France hears a hundred times a day, whether she is passing by on a bicycle with her skirts whipped by the wind or on the sidewalk with fresh makeup. A new hat, a bright dress, bare arms or legs, and immediately you hear, *oh là là.* After a while it's quite irritating.

Louki means, I don't know why, *regarder* [look at], probably like our *zyeuter* [stare], and is generally said twice: "*Louki, louki.*" The English airplane that comes to locate your position, the officer who comes to conduct an inspection, the fact of looking at something, whether directly or more or less from hiding, it's always, "*louki, louki.*"

A *mamoiselle* is the girl of your dreams, one that you have noticed passing by, or more simply the young maid-servant or sadly complaisant girl from whom a soldier hopes to obtain all the simple and inevitable pleasures.

A nice village or a splendid camp is a place where there are *beaucoup mamoiselle*. And it's the first question that's asked you, in all simplicity, by the crew-cut trooper when he arrives at your house: "*Beaucoup mamoiselle?*" and he makes a wide gesture to indicate the village. Alas, you can tell him yes with assurance! In the evening when he sadly makes his patrol he tells you, "No good, no *mamoiselle*," or even, "War not good, not *beaucoup mamoiselle*." In short it is, if you want to call it that, *l'amour*. Alas!

Grand filou! [big rogue] is a gentle insult or a sign of anger, depending on how it's said. A girl jostled and followed too closely says, with a stupidly annoyed air and a smile that belies it, "*Grand filou*." But if a soldier steals something from you, you can say to him with contempt, "German soldier, *grand filou*," and he will understand that you are not at all happy and that perhaps there's going to be trouble.

There is *beaucoup*, which applies, naturally, to everything: *beaucoup* work, *beaucoup* kilometers when it's a long distance, *beaucoup* money when something is expensive, *beaucoup* angry, *beaucoup* sick, etc.

And the eternal, indispensable dirty word, said in German with the appropriate conviction, is *cheis* (spelling?) [*Scheiss*], which one ends up saying too, let's admit it, from hearing it so much. The big crew-cut twenty-year-old boy who is a good sort but always grumbles, says it continually; and for it to be better and more strongly expressed, the better to get it off his chest, he continually spits out: "*Cheis, cheis, beaucoup merde* [shit]!" That way, everybody understands!

FOOTNOTES

1. Cariole: A small, open two-wheeled vehicle.

2. N.C.O.: non-commissioned officer. An enlisted member of the armed forces appointed to rank conferring leadership over other men.

3. Requistion slip: an official German document confirming a mandate to commandeer personnel, housing, supplies, etc., for redistribution to and use by occupying forces. The slips always passed through the mayor's office for his signature.

4. Spiess: Army slang for "top sergeant"; not military rank, properly speaking.

5. In French, April Fool is *Poisson d'Avril*, literally, "April Fish"; thus the joke of secretly hanging a paper cutout of a fish on someone's back, like a KICK ME sign.

6. *Grand malheur*: See author's glossary (page 114).
   Kaput: See author's glossary (page 114).

7. A.A.: Anti-aircraft firing (in French, D.C.A. or Défense Contre Avions).

8. Brière: Brière, a Frenchman, lived in Caen and was infamous and despised for turning in his countrymen to the Gestapo. According to one story, people in Caen would throw cheese from second- and third-story windows to passing Germans below, and for this crime Brière would report them to the Gestapo.

9. The Afrika [Korps], known as the German Africa Corps in English.

10. Though Marie-Louise Osmont was Catholic, her husband, Maurice, was Protestant, and the Osmonts kept their household as Protestant, which was quite unusual for the primarily Catholic region.

11. Tommies: British soldiers (from "Tommy Atkins," originally a fictitious name used in sample forms for privates in the British army).

12. *Boche*: A derogatory term used by the French to describe German individuals or the German people in general; also used as an adjective.

13. The Cotentin is the end portion of the peninsula, where Cherbourg is located. It is in the department of the Manche.

14. The H.M.S. *Ramillies*.

15. *Bon Sauveur*: Good Savior. Refers to both a hospital and an area of the city.

16. La Miséricorde: Mercy Hospital.

17. D.P. (Défense Passive): A French civilian recruit sanctioned as a caretaker of the French citizens. A D.P.'s duties varied from caring for the French wounded to covering tiled roofs with blue paper to reduce the chance of being bombed.

A Note on the Type

This book was set in a digitized version of Goudy Old Style.
The original font was designed by one of America's
premier type designers, Frederic W. Goudy.
He designed it for the American Type Founders in 1915.
The capitals were inspired from lettering in a painting
by Renaissance painter Holbein.